2541839

This bo
latest da
of the p

DATE

'1 1 M

D1134189

THE NEW TEMPLE SHAKESPEARE

Edited by M. R. Ridley, M.A.

KING HENRY VI
THIRD PART
by William Shakespeare

London: J. M. DENT & SONS LTD.
New York: E. P. DUTTON & CO. INC.

Editor's General Note

The Text. The editor has kept before him the aim of presenting to the modern reader the nearest possible approximation to what Shakespeare actually wrote. The text is therefore conservative, and is based on the earliest reliable printed text. But to avoid distraction (*a*) the spelling is modernised, and (*b*) a limited number of universally accepted emendations is admitted without comment. Where a Quarto text exists as well as the First Folio the passages which occur only in the Quarto are enclosed in square brackets [ ] and those which occur only in the Folio in brace brackets { }.

Scene Division. The rapid continuity of the Elizabethan curtainless production is lost by the 'traditional' scene divisions. Where there is an essential difference of place these scene divisions are retained. Where on the other hand the change of place is insignificant the scene division is indicated only by a space on the page. For ease of reference, however, the 'traditional' division is retained at the head of the page and in line numbering.

Notes. Passages on which there are notes are indicated by a † in the margin.

Punctuation adheres more closely than has been usual to the 'Elizabethan' punctuation of the early texts. It is often therefore more indicative of the way in which the lines were to be delivered than of their syntactical construction.

Glossaries are arranged on a somewhat novel principle, not alphabetically, but in the order in which the words or phrases occur. The editor is much indebted to Mr J. N. Bryson for his collaboration in the preparation of the glossaries.

Preface

The Text. The textual problem presented by the second and third parts of *Henry VI* is quite different from that presented by the first part, and greatly more complex. In 1594 appeared a Quarto, printed by Thomas Creed for Thomas Millington, entitled: 'The First part of the Contention betwixt the two famous Houses of Yorke and Lancaster, with the death of the good Duke Humphrey: And the banishment and death of the Duke of *Suffolke*, and the Tragicall end of the proud Cardinall of *Winchester*, with the notable Rebellion of *Iacke Cade: And the Duke of Yorkes first claime unto the Crowne*.' And in the next year appeared another Quarto, from the same publisher, 'The true Tragedie of Richard *Duke of Yorke, and the death of* good King Henrie the Sixt, *with the whole contention betweene* the two Houses Lancaster and Yorke, as it was sundrie times acted by the Right Honourable the Earle of Pembroke his seruants.' That there is some relation between these two quartos and the second and third parts of *Henry VI* as printed in the Folio is obvious; but what that relation is has been the subject of vigorous and often acrimonious dispute. One view (which may be called the 'foundation-play' view) is represented by Grant White's theory that 'the First Part of the Contention, The True Tragedy— and, probably, an early form of the First Part of *King Henry the Sixth* unknown to us, were written by Marlowe, Greene, and Shakespeare (and perhaps Peele) together, not improbably as co-labourers for the company known as the Earl of Pembroke's servants, soon after the arrival of Shakespeare in London; and that he, in taking passages, and sometimes whole scenes, from those plays,

vii

for his *King Henry the Sixth*, did little more than to reclaim his own.' The other view (which may be called the 'Bad-Quarto' view) was summarised (not without courage, considering the trend of Shakespearean scholarship of his time) by Halliwell-Phillipps: 'The theory which best agrees with the positive evidences is that which concedes the authorship of the three plays [1. 2. 3. *Henry VI*] to Shakespeare, their production to the year 1592, and the quarto editions of the Second and Third Parts as vamped, imperfect, and blundering versions of the poet's own original dramas.' This view was handled by Furnivall in the best manner of robustious controversy. 'This,' said Furnivall, 'is surely a refuge for the brain-destitute. And if any want-wit can bring what he is pleased to call his mind, to accept for a time this notion of the authorship of *The Contention* and *True Tragedy*, he must be left to grow out of it.' But in 1929 Professor Alexander, in a most able study of the problem,[1] with considerably more urbanity than Furnivall, through with an equal conviction of the destitution of brain in the opposite camp, raised the 'Bad-Quarto' view to something near a certainty. I should hesitate to say that Professor Alexander has proved his point, since he suffers, I think, from a tendency to assume as a premise in his argument the very conclusion which by the argument he is trying to prove,[2] and he does not seem to me wholly convincing (nor indeed himself wholly at ease) in his treatment of certain

[1] *Shakespeare's Henry VI and Richard III.*

[2] For example, quite early in the argument we find the statement with regard to the Quarto that 'Warwick's part all through is outstanding for its accuracy.' We have no right to speak of accuracy unless we know in advance that F is the original from which Q was taken. The observable facts are simply that there is a close degree of correspondence between the part of Warwick as given in Q and the same part as given in F, from which, taken in isolation, we might just as legitimately argue that F was an 'accurate' reproduction of Q.

minor issues.[1] But he has at any rate cleared the ground of a deal of lumber of misinterpretation, and set out with great clarity the evidence which the reader can handle for himself, even when he thinks that Professor Alexander's own handling is a trifle over-confident. To me the evidence is, on the main issue, and at any rate with regard to Part II, entirely convincing. There can, I think, be little doubt that *The Contention* is a 'reported text'[2] (using the term in its widest sense) of an original which is represented with at least a high degree of completeness and fidelity by the Folio. Nor can I see any necessity for assuming either that Shakespeare was rehandling material provided by contemporary dramatists (quite apart from the improbability, well argued by Professor Alexander, of his doing anything of the kind) or that he had a collaborator. Much of the supposed 'evidence' of parallels is disposed of the moment we accept the theory of a 'reported text,' and for the rest we do well to remember a wise remark of Sir Edmund Chambers, 'I do not think we have adequate criteria for distinguishing with any assurance from the style of his contemporaries that of a young writer still under their influence.' The second and third parts of

---

[1] For example, the odd coincidence in certain stage-directions between the two texts, a coincidence not too easy to account for, and the assumption of a transcript being by some accident available for a few small portions of Q. As also the cavalier treatment of Jaggard's reprint of 1619, of which Professor Alexander says, 'That Jaggard had no manuscript at his disposal is a fair inference from the corrections he made.' If corrections is understood in its narrowest sense this may be true, but there are two remarkable additions in the second scene of *The Contention*, one of a line and a half and one of three lines and a half, both of which correspond (though roughly) to F, and which it is hard to suppose that Jaggard or Jaggard's compositor inserted out of his head.

[2] A 'reported' text in the widest sense need not be one constructed from a shorthand report; it may be one constructed by memorisation, with or without the assistance of one or more of the actors (in this case, according to Alexander, the actor who played Warwick and the actor who doubled Suffolk and Clifford).

the play seem to me here on a different plane from the first part. In the first part I agree with Professor Alexander that it is absurd to suppose that because in a historical play different sections deal with different blocks of historical events there is even a prima facie probability that those different blocks were handled by different writers: but I am also aware of jolts, of a kind of geological 'fault' in the strata, that make it hard for me to suppose that the whole play was written by one writer, unless at very different times. But the personal equation is the poorest sort of evidence, and in any case I think that few readers will be aware of any such 'faults' in the second and third parts. I still regard the Folio as more of an 'edited' text than I think Professor Alexander would be prepared to admit (though I should take the 'editing,' if it occurred, as evidence rather of Heminge and Condell's piety than their dishonesty), and I am prepared therefore to believe that the Folio text has been somewhat 'improved' from its original. And for this reason, and as a matter of interest, I have given a few of the Q versions, whether in the text or the notes.[1] But in the upshot it seems to me clear that the editor of such an edition as this need concern himself and his readers only with the Folio text; and that both he and they can with clear consciences assume that in dealing with that text they are dealing with Shakespeare rather than with a committee.

(I have here given only a conclusion. Any reader who wishes to pursue the topic, which is of the highest interest for the student of the 'determination of Shakespeare's text' but of less interest for the reader of Shakespeare, must be referred to Professor Alexander's study, and also to the Sir Edmund Chambers' *William Shakespeare*,

---

[1] Where a passage in brace brackets { } is followed immediately by one in square brackets, that, in this play, is no more than a method of indicating the extent of the F passage to which the Q parallel is being given.

i. 277-93, who, though accepting the 'reported text' theory in the main, raises some very pertinent problems.

Nor have I entered into the reasons which make me less certain of Professor Alexander's conclusions with regard to Part III than with regard to Part II. To state them at all adequately would require a detailed examination of the available evidence quite beyond the scope of such a preface as this. Very briefly, the *True Tragedy*, as a whole, is much closer to F than *The Contention* is, and there are such long passages where the resemblance amounts so nearly to identity that one begins to think that the reporting—if it was reporting—must have been of uncommon accuracy, and to harbour an uneasy suspicion that for at any rate a good deal of the play there may have been a common MS. original. That is, if the *True Tragedy* stood alone the 'reported text' view would be, I think, less easy to substantiate. But, granted a certain antecedent probability that the text of both Quartos was arrived at by the same means, I think it more than likely that Professor Alexander is right about both.)

Date of Composition. One can only say, on grounds both of general probability and of style, later than Part I, and not much later.

Source. Again, as for Part I, Holinshed (Halle) in the first place. There are traces of indebtedness to Fabyan, Grafton, and Stowe. (See Boswell-Stone, *Shakespeare's Holinshed*.)

Duration of Action. For the third part Daniel gives twenty days, with intervals suggesting two months. The historic time is 1455-1471.

Criticism.

Hazlitt.—During the time of the civil wars of York and Lancaster, England was a perfect bear-garden, and Shakespear has given us a very lively picture of the scene. The three parts of *Henry VI* convey a picture of very little else: and are inferior to the other historical plays. They have brilliant passages: but the general groundwork is comparatively poor and meagre, the style 'flat and unraised.'

Dowden.—Among his 'wolfish Earls' Henry is in constant terror, not of being himself torn to pieces, but of their flying at one another's throats. Violent scenes, disturbing the cloistral peace which it would please him to see reign throughout the universe, are hateful and terrible to Henry. He rides out hawking with his Queen and Suffolk, the Cardinal and Gloster; some of the riders hardly able for an hour to conceal their emulation and their hate. Henry takes a languid interest in the sport, but all occasions supply food for his contemplative piety; he suffers from a certain incontinence of devout feeling, and now the falcons set him moralising. A moment after, and the peers, with Margaret among them, are bandying furious words. Henry's anguish is extreme, but he hopes that something may be done by a few moral reflections suitable to the occasion.

KING HENRY VI

THIRD PART

DRAMATIS PERSONÆ

KING HENRY *the sixth*.
EDWARD, *Prince of Wales, his son*.
LOUIS XI, *King of France*.
DUKE OF SOMERSET.
DUKE OF EXETER.
EARL OF OXFORD.
EARL OF NORTHUMBERLAND.
EARL OF WESTMORELAND.
LORD CLIFFORD.
RICHARD PLANTAGENET, *Duke of York*.
EDWARD, *Earl of March, afterwards King Edward IV*, \
EDMUND, *Earl of Rutland*,   } *his*
GEORGE, *afterwards Duke of Clarence*,   } *sons*.
RICHARD, *afterwards Duke of Gloucester*, /
DUKE OF NORFOLK.
MARQUESS OF MONTAGUE.
EARL OF WARWICK.
EARL OF PEMBROKE.
LORD HASTINGS.
LORD STAFFORD.
SIR JOHN MORTIMER,   } *uncles to the Duke of York*.
SIR HUGH MORTIMER, /
HENRY, *Earl of Richmond, a youth*.
LORD RIVERS, *brother to Lady Grey*.
SIR WILLIAM STANLEY.
SIR JOHN MONTGOMERY.
SIR JOHN SOMERVILLE.
Tutor to Rutland.   Mayor of York.
Lieutenant of the Tower.   A Nobleman.
Two Keepers.   A Huntsman.
A Son that has killed his father.
A Father that has killed his son.

QUEEN MARGARET.
LADY GREY, *afterwards Queen to Edward IV*.
BONA, *sister to the French Queen*.

Soldiers, Attendants, Messengers, Watchmen, &c.

SCENE: *England and France*.

THE THIRD PART OF
KING HENRY VI

Act First

SCENE I

London. The Parliament-house

Alarum. Enter the Duke of York, Edward, Richard, Norfolk, Montague, Warwick, and Soldiers [with white roses in their hats]

*War.*I wonder how the king escap'd our hands.
Yo. While we pursued the horsemen of the north,
He slily stole away, and left his men:
Whereat the great Lord of Northumberland,
Whose warlike ears could never brook retreat,
Cheer'd up the drooping army, and himself,
Lord Clifford, and Lord Stafford, all a-breast,
Charg'd our main battle's front, and breaking in
Were by the swords of common soldiers slain.
*Edw.*Lord Stafford's father, Duke of Buckingham,   10
Is either slain or wounded dangerously;
I cleft his beaver with a downright blow:

1

That this is true, father, behold his blood.

Mon. And, brother, here's the Earl of Wiltshire's blood,
Whom I encounter'd as the battles join'd.

Ric. Speak thou for me, and tell them what I did.

Throwing down the Duke of Somerset's head

Yo. Richard hath best deserv'd of all my sons:
But is your grace dead, my Lord of Somerset?

Nor. Such hope have all the line of John of Gaunt!

Ric. Thus do I hope to shake King Henry's head.   20

War. And so do I, victorious Prince of York:
Before I see thee seated in that throne
Which now the house of Lancaster usurps,
I vow by heaven, these eyes shall never close.
This is the palace of the fearful king,
And this the regal seat: possess it, York,
For this is thine, and not King Henry's heirs'.

Yo. Assist me, then, sweet Warwick, and I will,
For hither we have broken in by force.

Nor. We'll all assist you; he that flies shall die.   30

Yo. Thanks, gentle Norfolk: stay by me, my lords;
And, soldiers, stay and lodge by me this night.

They go up

War. And when the king comes, offer him no violence,
Unless he seek to thrust you out perforce.

Yo. The queen this day here holds her parliament,

2

But little thinks we shall be of her council :
By words or blows here let us win our right.

Ric. Arm'd as we are, let's stay within this house.

War. The bloody parliament shall this be call'd,
Unless Plantagenet, Duke of York, be king,   40
And bashful Henry depos'd, whose cowardice
Hath made us by-words to our enemies.

Yo. Then leave me not, my lords, be resolute ;
I mean to take possession of my right.

War. Neither the king, nor he that loves him best,
The proudest he that holds up Lancaster,
Dares stir a wing, if Warwick shake his bells.
I'll plant Plantagenet, root him up who dares :
Resolve thee, Richard ; claim the English crown.

*Flourish. Enter King Henry, Clifford, Northumberland, West-
moreland, Exeter, and the rest [with red roses in their hats]*

K.H. My lords, look where the sturdy rebel sits,   50
Even in the chair of state : belike he means,
Back'd by the power of Warwick, that false peer,
To aspire unto the crown and reign as king.
Earl of Northumberland, he slew thy father,
And thine, Lord Clifford ; and you both have vow'd
      revenge
On him, his sons, his favourites, and his friends.

Nor. If I be not, heavens be reveng'd on me !

Cli. The hope thereof makes Clifford mourn in steel.

Wes. What, shall we suffer this ? let's pluck him down,
My heart for anger burns, I cannot brook it. 60

K.H. Be patient, gentle Earl of Westmoreland.

Cli. Patience is for poltroons, such as he :
He durst not sit there, had your father liv'd.
My gracious lord, here in the parliament
Let us assail the family of York.

Nor. Well hast thou spoken, cousin, be it so.

K.H. Ah, know you not the city favours them,
And they have troops of soldiers at their beck ?

Exe. But when the duke is slain, they'll quickly fly.

K.H. Far be the thought of this from Henry's heart, 70
To make a shambles of the parliament-house !
Cousin of Exeter, frowns, words and threats
Shall be the war that Henry means to use.
Thou factious Duke of York, descend my throne,
And kneel for grace and mercy at my feet ;
I am thy sovereign.

Yo. [Thou art deceiv'd ;] I am thine.

Exe. For shame, come down : he made thee Duke of York.

Yo. 'Twas my inheritance, as the earldom was. †

Exe. Thy father was a traitor to the crown.

War. Exeter, thou art a traitor to the crown, 80
In following this usurping Henry.

Cli. Whom should he follow but his natural king?

War. True, Clifford; and that's Richard Duke of York.

K.H. And shall I stand, and thou sit in my throne?

Yo. It must and shall be so, content thyself.

War. Be Duke of Lancaster, let him be king.

Wes. He is both king and Duke of Lancaster,
And that the Lord of Westmoreland shall maintain.

War. And Warwick shall disprove it.   You forget
That we are those which chas'd you from the field,   90
And slew your fathers, and with colours spread
March'd through the city to the palace gates.

Nor. Yes, Warwick, I remember it to my grief,
And, by his soul, thou and thy house shall rue it.

Wes. Plantagenet, of thee and these thy sons,
Thy kinsmen and thy friends, I'll have more lives
Than drops of blood were in my father's veins.

Cli. Urge it no more, lest that, instead of words,
I send thee, Warwick, such a messenger
As shall revenge his death before I stir.   100

War. Poor Clifford! how I scorn his worthless threats!

Yo. Will you we show our title to the crown?
If not, our swords shall plead it in the field.

K.H. What title hast thou, traitor, to the crown?
Thy father was, as thou art, Duke of York;
Thy grandfather, Roger Mortimer, Earl of March:

5

  I am the son of Henry the Fifth,
  Who made the Dauphin and the French to stoop,
  And seiz'd upon their towns and provinces.

War. Talk not of France, sith thou hast lost it all.   110

K.H. The lord protector lost it, and not I :
  When I was crown'd I was but nine months old.

Ric. You are old enough now, and yet, methinks, you lose.
  Father, tear the crown from the usurper's head.

Edw. Sweet father, do so ; set it on your head.

Mon. Good brother, as thou lov'st and honourest arms,
  Let's fight it out, and not stand cavilling thus.

Ric. Sound drums and trumpets, and the king will fly.

Yo. Sons, peace !

K.H. Peace, thou ! and give King Henry leave to speak.   120

{*War.* Plantagenet shall speak first : hear him, lords,
  And be you silent and attentive too,
  For he that interrupts him shall not live.}

K.H. [Ah, Plantagenet, why seek'st thou to depose me ?
  Are we not both Plantagenets by birth
  And from two brothers lineally descent ?
  Suppose by right and equity thou be king,]
  Think'st thou that I will leave my kingly throne,
  Wherein my grandsire and my father sat ?
  No : first shall war unpeople this my realm ;
  Ay, and their colours, often borne in France,

And now in England to our heart's great sorrow,
Shall be my winding-sheet.   Why faint you, lords ?
My title 's good, and better far than his.   130

*War.*Prove it, Henry, and thou shalt be king.

*K.H.*Henry the Fourth by conquest got the crown.

Yo. 'Twas by rebellion against his king.

K.H.(*aside*) I know not what to say ; my title 's weak.
Tell me, may not a king adopt an heir ?

Yo. What then ?

*K.H.*An if he may, then am I lawful king ;
For Richard, in the view of many lords,
Resign'd the crown to Henry the Fourth,
Whose heir my father was, and I am his.   140

Yo. He rose against him, being his sovereign,
And made him to resign his crown perforce.

*War.*Suppose, my lords, he did it unconstrain'd,
Think you 'twere prejudicial to his crown ?

*Exe.*No ; for he could not so resign his crown
But that the next heir should succeed and reign.

*K.H.*Art thou against us, Duke of Exeter ?

*Exe.*His is the right, and therefore pardon me.

Yo. Why whisper you, my lords, and answer not ?

*Exe.*My conscience tells me he is lawful king.   150

K.H.(*aside*) All will revolt from me, and turn to him.

*Nor.*Plantagenet, for all the claim thou lay'st,

7

Think not that Henry shall be so depos'd.

War. Depos'd he shall be, in despite of all.

Nor. Thou art deceiv'd : 'tis not thy southern power,
Of Essex, Norfolk, Suffolk, nor of Kent,
Which makes thee thus presumptuous and proud,
Can set the duke up in despite of me.

Cli. King Henry, be thy title right or wrong,
Lord Clifford vows to fight in thy defence :   160
May that ground gape and swallow me alive,
Where I shall kneel to him that slew my father !

K.H. O Clifford, how thy words revive my heart !

Yo. Henry of Lancaster, resign thy crown.
What mutter you, or what conspire you, lords ?

War. Do right unto this princely Duke of York,
Or I will fill the house with armed men,
And over the chair of state, where now he sits,
Write up his title with usurping blood.

He stamps with his foot, and the Soldiers show themselves

K.H. My Lord of Warwick, hear me but one word :   170
Let me for this my life-time reign as king.

Yo. Confirm the crown to me and to mine heirs,
And thou shalt reign in quiet while thou liv'st.

{*K.H.* I am content : Richard Plantagenet,
Enjoy the kingdom after my decease.}

[*K.H.* Convey the soldiers hence, and then I will.

*War.*Captain, conduct them unto Tuthill fields.]

Cli. What wrong is this unto the prince your son !

*War.*What good is this to England and himself !

*Wes.*Base, fearful and despairing Henry !

Cli. How hast thou injur'd both thyself and us !

*Wes.*I cannot stay to hear these articles.   180

*Nor.*Nor I.

Cli. Come, cousin, let us tell the queen these news.

*Wes.*Farewell, faint-hearted and degenerate king,

    In whose cold blood no spark of honour bides.

*Nor.*Be thou a prey unto the house of York,

    And die in bands for this unmanly deed !   †

Cli. In dreadful war mayst thou be overcome,

    Or live in peace abandon'd and despis'd !

                Exeunt Nor., Clif., and Wes.

*War.*Turn this way, Henry, and regard them not.

*Exe.*They seek revenge, and therefore will not yield.   190

*K.H.*Ah, Exeter !

War.   Why should you sigh, my lord ?

*K.H.*Not for myself, Lord Warwick, but my son,

    Whom I unnaturally shall disinherit.

    But be it as it may : I here entail

    The crown to thee and to thine heirs for ever,

    Conditionally, that here thou take an oath

    To cease this civil war ; and, whilst I live,

     To honour me as thy king and sovereign,
     And neither by treason nor hostility
     To seek to put me down and reign thyself.   200

Yo. This oath I willingly take, and will perform.

War. Long live King Henry ! Plantagenet, embrace him.

K.H. And long live thou and these thy forward sons !

Yo. Now York and Lancaster are reconcil'd.

Exe. Accurs'd be he that seeks to make them foes !

                Sennet. Here they come down

Yo. Farewell, my gracious lord, I 'll to my castle.

War. And I 'll keep London with my soldiers.

Nor. And I to Norfolk with my followers.

Mon. And I unto the sea from whence I came.

      Exeunt York and his Sons, Warwick, Norfolk,
            Montague, their Soldiers, and Attendants

K.H. And I, with grief and sorrow, to the court.   210

     Enter Queen Margaret and the Prince of Wales

Exe. Here comes the queen, whose looks bewray her anger :
     I 'll steal away.

K.H.   Exeter, so will I.

Mar. Nay, go not from me, I will follow thee.

K.H. Be patient, gentle queen, and I will stay.

Mar. Who can be patient in such extremes ?

     Ah, wretched man ! would I had died a maid,
     And never seen thee, never borne thee son,

Seeing thou hast prov'd so unnatural a father!
Hath he deserv'd to lose his birthright thus?
Hadst thou but lov'd him half so well as I,　　　220
Or felt that pain which I did for him once,
Or nourish'd him, as I did with my blood,
Thou wouldst have left thy dearest heart-blood there,
Rather than have made that savage duke thine heir,
And disinherited thine only son.

Pri. Father, you cannot disinherit me:
If you be king, why should not I succeed?

K.H. Pardon me, Margaret, pardon me, sweet son;
The Earl of Warwick and the duke enforc'd me.

Mar. Enforc'd thee? art thou king, and wilt be forc'd?　　230
I shame to hear thee speak.   Ah, timorous wretch!
Thou hast undone thyself, thy son, and me,
And given unto the house of York such head,
As thou shalt reign but by their sufferance.
To entail him and his heirs unto the crown,
What is it, but to make thy sepulchre,
And creep into it far before thy time?
Warwick is chancellor, and the lord of Calais,
Stern Falconbridge commands the narrow seas,
The duke is made protector of the realm,　　　240
And yet shalt thou be safe? such safety finds
The trembling lamb, environed with wolves.

Had I been there, which am a silly woman,
The soldiers should have toss'd me on their pikes,
Before I would have granted to that act.
But thou preferr'st thy life before thine honour:
And seeing thou dost, I here divorce myself
Both from thy table, Henry, and thy bed,
Until that act of parliament be repeal'd,
Whereby my son is disinherited.   250
The northern lords that have forsworn thy colours
Will follow mine, if once they see them spread;
And spread they shall be, to thy foul disgrace
And utter ruin of the house of York.
Thus do I leave thee.   Come, son, let's away;
Our army is ready; come, we'll after them.

*K.H.*Stay, gentle Margaret, and hear me speak.

*Mar.*Thou hast spoke too much already: get thee gone.

*K.H.*Gentle son Edward, thou wilt stay with me?

*Mar.*Ay, to be murder'd by his enemies.   260

Pri. When I return with victory from the field
I'll see your grace: till then I'll follow her.

*Mar.*Come, son, away, we may not linger thus.

> *Exeunt Queen Margaret and the Prince*

*K.H.*Poor queen! how love to me and to her son
Hath made her break out into terms of rage!
Reveng'd may she be on that hateful duke,

12

Whose haughty spirit, winged with desire,
Will cost my crown, and like an empty eagle
Tire on the flesh of me and of my son !
The loss of those three lords torments my heart :   270
I'll write unto them, and entreat them fair.
Come, cousin, you shall be the messenger.

Exe. And I, I hope, shall reconcile them all.   *Exeunt*

SCENE II

Sandal Castle

Enter Richard, Edward, and Montague

Ric. Brother, though I be youngest, give me leave.
Edw. No, I can better play the orator.
Mon. But I have reasons strong and forcible.

Enter the Duke of York

Yo. Why, how now, sons and brother ? at a strife ?
   What is your quarrel ? how began it first ?
Edw. No quarrel, but a slight contention.   †
Yo. About what ?
Ric. About that which concerns your grace and us,
   The crown of England, father, which is yours.
Yo. Mine, boy ? not till King Henry be dead.   10
Ric. Your right depends not on his life or death.

13

Edw. Now you are heir, therefore enjoy it now:
　　By giving the house of Lancaster leave to breathe,
　　It will outrun you, father, in the end.

Yo. I took an oath, that he should quietly reign.

Edw. But for a kingdom any oath may be broken:
　　I would break a thousand oaths to reign one year.

Ric. No; God forbid your grace should be forsworn.

Yo. I shall be, if I claim by open war.

Ric. I'll prove the contrary, if you'll hear me speak.　　20

Yo. Thou canst not, son; it is impossible.

Ric. An oath is of no moment, being not took
　　Before a true and lawful magistrate,
　　That hath authority over him that swears:
　　Henry had none, but did usurp the place;
　　Then, seeing 'twas he that made you to depose,
　　Your oath, my lord, is vain and frivolous.
　　Therefore, to arms! And, father, do but think
　　How sweet a thing it is to wear a crown;
　　Within whose circuit is Elysium,　　30
　　And all that poets feign of bliss and joy.
　　Why do we linger thus? I cannot rest
　　Until the white rose that I wear be dyed
　　Even in the lukewarm blood of Henry's heart.

Yo. Richard, enough; I will be king, or die.
　　Brother, thou shalt to London presently,

And whet on Warwick to this enterprise.
Thou, Richard, shalt to the Duke of Norfolk,
And tell him privily of our intent.
You, Edward, shall unto my Lord Cobham,   40
With whom the Kentishmen will willingly rise :
In them I trust ; for they are soldiers,
Witty, courteous, liberal, full of spirit.
While you are thus employ'd, what resteth more,
But that I seek occasion how to rise,
And yet the king not privy to my drift,
Nor any of the house of Lancaster ?

Enter a Messenger

But, stay : what news ?   Why com'st thou in such
    post ?
Mes. The queen with all the northern earls and lords
Intend here to besiege you in your castle :   50
She is hard by, with twenty thousand men ;
And therefore fortify your hold, my lord.
Yo. Ay, with my sword.   What ? think'st thou that we
    fear them ?
Edward and Richard, you shall stay with me,
My brother Montague, shall post to London :
Let noble Warwick, Cobham, and the rest,
Whom we have left protectors of the king,
With powerful policy strengthen themselves,

      And trust not simple Henry nor his oaths.

*Mon.*Brother, I go ; I 'll win them, fear it not :   60
      And thus most humbly I do take my leave.   *Exit*
      Enter Sir John Mortimer and Sir Hugh Mortimer

Yo. Sir John and Sir Hugh Mortimer, mine uncles,
      You are come to Sandal in a happy hour ;
      The army of the queen mean to besiege us.

*J.M.*She shall not need, we 'll meet her in the field.

Yo. What, with five thousand men ?

Ric. Ay, with five hundred, father, for a need :
      A woman 's general ; what should we fear ?

                            A march afar off

*Edw.*I hear their drums : let 's set our men in order,
      And issue forth and bid them battle straight.   70

Yo. Five men to twenty ! though the odds be great,
      I doubt not, uncle, of our victory.
      Many a battle have I won in France,
      Whenas the enemy hath been ten to one :
      Why should I not now have the like success ?

                            Alarum. Exeunt

SCENE III

Field of battle betwixt Sandal Castle and Wakefield

Alarums. Enter Rutland and his Tutor

Tut. [O fly, my lord, let's leave the Castle,
    And fly to Wakefield straight.]

Rut. {Ah, whither shall I fly to 'scape their hands?}
    Ah, tutor, look where bloody Clifford comes!

Enter Clifford and Soldiers

Cli. Chaplain, away! thy priesthood saves thy life.
    As for the brat of this accursed duke,
    Whose father slew my father, he shall die.

Tut. And I, my lord, will bear him company.

Cli. Soldiers, away with him!

Tut. Ah, Clifford, murder not this innocent child,
    Lest thou be hated both of God and man!

Exit, dragged off by Soldiers

Cli. How now? is he dead already? or is it fear   10
    That makes him close his eyes? I'll open them.

Rut. So looks the pent-up lion o'er the wretch
    That trembles under his devouring paws;
    And so he walks, insulting o'er his prey,
    And so he comes, to rend his limbs asunder.
    Ah, gentle Clifford, kill me with thy sword,

17

And not with such a cruel threatening look.
Sweet Clifford, hear me speak before I die.
I am too mean a subject for thy wrath :
Be thou reveng'd on men, and let me live.   20

Cli. In vain thou speak'st, poor boy ; my father's blood
Hath stopp'd the passage where thy words should
    enter.

Rut. Then let my father's blood open it again :
He is a man, and, Clifford, cope with him.

Cli. Had I thy brethren here, their lives and thine
Were not revenge sufficient for me ;
No, if I digg'd up thy forefathers' graves,
And hung their rotten coffins up in chains,
It could not slake mine ire, nor ease my heart.
The sight of any of the house of York   30
Is as a fury to torment my soul ;
And till I root out their accursed line
And leave not one alive, I live in hell.
Therefore—   *Lifting his hand*

Rut. O, let me pray before I take my death !
To thee I pray ; sweet Clifford, pity me !

Cli. Such pity as my rapier's point affords.

Rut. I never did thee harm : why wilt thou slay me ?

Cli. Thy father hath.

Rut.   But 'twas ere I was born.

Thou hast one son, for his sake pity me,   40
Lest in revenge thereof, sith God is just,
He be as miserably slain as I.
Ah, let me live in prison all my days,
And when I give occasion of offence,
Then let me die, for now thou hast no cause.

Cli. No cause ?
Thy father slew my father ; therefore die.   *Stabs him*

Rut. Di faciant laudis summa sit ista tuæ !   *Dies*

Cli. Plantagenet ! I come, Plantagenet !
And this thy son's blood cleaving to my blade   50
Shall rust upon my weapon, till thy blood,
Congeal'd with this, do make me wipe off both.   †

                                        Exit

SCENE IV

Another part of the field

Alarum.   Enter Richard, Duke of York

Yo. The army of the queen hath got the field :
My uncles both are slain, in rescuing me ;
And all my followers to the eager foe
Turn back, and fly, like ships before the wind,
Or lambs pursued by hunger-starved wolves.

My sons, God knows what hath bechanced them:
But this I know, they have demean'd themselves
Like men born to renown, by life or death.
Three times did Richard make a lane to me,
And thrice cried 'Courage, father! fight it out!'   10
And full as oft came Edward to my side,
With purple falchion, painted to the hilt
In blood of those that had encounter'd him:
And when the hardiest warriors did retire,
Richard cried, 'Charge! and give no foot of ground!'
And cried, 'A crown, or else a glorious tomb!
A sceptre, or an earthly sepulchre!'
With this, we charg'd again: but, out, alas!
We bodg'd again, as I have seen a swan
With bootless labour swim against the tide,   20
And spend her strength with over-matching waves.

A short alarum within

Ah, hark! the fatal followers do pursue,
And I am faint, and cannot fly their fury:
And were I strong, I would not shun their fury:
The sands are number'd that make up my life,
Here must I stay, and here my life must end.

*Enter Queen Margaret, Clifford, Northumberland,
the young Prince, and Soldiers*

Come, bloody Clifford, rough Northumberland,

I dare your quenchless fury to more rage ;
I am your butt, and I abide your shot.

Nor. Yield to our mercy, proud Plantagenet.   30
Cli. Ay, to such mercy as his ruthless arm,
    With downright payment, show'd unto my father.
    Now Phaëthon hath tumbled from his car,   †
    And made an evening at the noontide prick.
Yo. My ashes as the phœnix, may bring forth
    A bird that will revenge upon you all :
    And in that hope I throw mine eyes to heaven,
    Scorning whate'er you can afflict me with.
    Why come you not ? what ? multitudes, and fear ?
Cli. So cowards fight when they can fly no further,   40
    So doves do peck the falcon's piercing talons,
    So desperate thieves, all hopeless of their lives,
    Breathe out invectives 'gainst the officers.
Yo. O Clifford, but bethink thee once again,
    And in thy thought o'er-run my former time ;
    And, if thou canst for blushing, view this face,
    And bite thy tongue, that slanders him with cowardice
    Whose frown hath made thee faint and fly ere this !
Cli. I will not bandy with thee word for word,
    But buckle with thee blows, twice two for one.   50
Mar. Hold, valiant Clifford ! for a thousand causes
    I would prolong awhile the traitor's life.

Wrath makes him deaf : speak thou, Northumberland.

Nor. Hold, Clifford ! do not honour him so much
To prick thy finger, though to wound his heart :
What valour were it, when a cur doth grin,
For one to thrust his hand between his teeth,
When he might spurn him with his foot away ?
It is war's prize to take all vantages ;
And ten to one is no impeach of valour.   60

They lay hands on York, who struggles

Cli. Ay, ay, so strives the woodcock with the gin.

Nor. So doth the cony struggle in the net.

Yo. So triumph thieves upon their conquer'd booty,
So true men yield, with robbers so o'er-match'd.

Nor. What would your grace have done unto him now ?

Mar. Brave warriors, Clifford and Northumberland,
Come, make him stand upon this molehill here,
That raught at mountains with outstretched arms,
Yet parted but the shadow with his hand.
What, was it you that would be England's king ?   70
Was't you that revell'd in our parliament,
And made a preachment of your high descent ?
Where are your mess of sons, to back you now ?
The wanton Edward, and the lusty George ?
And where 's that valiant crook-back prodigy,
Dicky your boy, that with his grumbling voice

Was wont to cheer his dad in mutinies ?
Or, with the rest, where is your darling Rutland ?
Look, York, I stain'd this napkin with the blood
That valiant Clifford, with his rapier's point,   80
Made issue from the bosom of the boy ;
And if thine eyes can water for his death,
I give thee this to dry thy cheeks withal.
Alas, poor York ! but that I hate thee deadly,
I should lament thy miserable state.
I prithee grieve, to make me merry, York.
What, hath thy fiery heart so parch'd thine entrails
That not a tear can fall for Rutland's death ?
Why art thou patient, man ? thou shouldst be mad ;
And I, to make thee mad, do mock thee thus.   90
Stamp, rave, and fret, that I may sing and dance.
Thou would'st be fee'd, I see, to make me sport :
York cannot speak, unless he wear a crown.
A crown for York ! and, lords, bow low to him :
Hold you his hands, whilst I do set it on.

                    Putting a paper crown on his head †
Ay, marry, sir, now looks he like a king !
Ay, this is he that took King Henry's chair,
And this is he was his adopted heir.
But how is it that great Plantagenet
Is crown'd so soon, and broke his solemn oath ?   100

As I bethink me, you should not be king
Till our King Henry had shook hands with death.
And will you pale your head in Henry's glory,
And rob his temples of the diadem,
Now in his life, against your holy oath ?
O, 'tis a fault too too unpardonable !
Off with the crown ; and, with the crown, his head,
And, whilst we breathe, take time to do him dead.

Cli. That is my office, for my father's sake.

Mar. Nay, stay, let 's hear the orisons he makes.   110

Yo. She-wolf of France, but worse than wolves of France,
Whose tongue more poisons than the adder's tooth !
How ill-beseeming is it in thy sex
To triumph like an Amazonian trull,
Upon their woes whom fortune captivates !
But that thy face is, visard-like, unchanging,
Made impudent with use of evil deeds,
I would assay, proud queen, to make thee blush.
To tell thee whence thou cam'st, of whom deriv'd,
Were shame enough to shame thee, wert thou not
    shameless.   120
Thy father bears the type of King of Naples,
Of both the Sicils, and Jerusalem,
Yet not so wealthy as an English yeoman.
Hath that poor monarch taught thee to insult ?

It needs not, nor it boots thee not, proud queen,
Unless the adage must be verified,
That beggars mounted run their horse to death.
'Tis beauty that doth oft make women proud,
But, God He knows, thy share thereof is small :
'Tis virtue that doth make them most admir'd,   130
The contrary doth make thee wonder'd at :
'Tis government that makes them seem divine,
The want thereof makes thee abominable :
Thou art as opposite to every good
As the Antipodes are unto us,
Or as the south to the septentrion.
O tiger's heart, wrapp'd in a woman's hide,   †
How couldst thou drain the life-blood of the child,
To bid the father wipe his eyes withal,
And yet be seen to bear a woman's face ?   140
Women are soft, mild, pitiful and flexible ;
Thou stern, obdurate, flinty, rough, remorseless.
Bid'st thou me rage ? why, now thou hast thy wish :
Wouldst have me weep ? why, now thou hast thy
     will :
For raging wind blows up incessant showers,
And when the rage allays, the rain begins.
These tears are my sweet Rutland's obsequies,
And every drop cries vengeance for his death,   †

'Gainst thee, fell Clifford, and thee, false French-
    woman.

Nor. Beshrew me, but his passion moves me so,   150
    That hardly can I check my eyes from tears.

Yo. That face of his the hungry cannibals
    Would not have touch'd, would not have stain'd
        with blood:
    But you are more inhuman, more inexorable,
    O, ten times more, than tigers of Hyrcania.   †
    See, ruthless queen, a hapless father's tears:
    This cloth thou dip'dst in blood of my sweet boy,
    And I with tears do wash the blood away.
    Keep thou the napkin, and go boast of this,
    And if thou tell'st the heavy story right,   160
    Upon my soul, the hearers will shed tears;
    Yea, even my foes will shed fast-falling tears,
    And say 'Alas, it was a piteous deed!'
    There, take the crown, and, with the crown, my curse;
    And in thy need such comfort come to thee
    As now I reap at thy too cruel hand!
    Hard-hearted Clifford, take me from the world,
    My soul to heaven, my blood upon your heads!

Nor. Had he been slaughter-man, to all my kin,
    I should not for my life but weep with him,   170
    To see how inly sorrow gripes his soul.

Mar. What, weeping-ripe, my Lord Northumberland ?
Think but upon the wrong he did us all,
And that will quickly dry thy melting tears.

Cli. Here 's for my oath, here 's for my father's death.

Stabbing him

Mar. And here 's to right our gentle-hearted king.

Stabbing him

Yo. Open Thy gate of mercy, gracious God !
My soul flies through these wounds, to seek out Thee.

Dies

Mar. Off with his head, and set it on York gates,
So York may overlook the town of York.   180

Flourish.   Exeunt

Act Second

SCENE I

A plain near Mortimer's Cross in Herefordshire

A march.   Enter Edward, Richard, and their power

Edw. I wonder how our princely father 'scap'd ;
Or whether he be 'scap'd away or no
From Clifford's and Northumberland's pursuit :

27

Had he been ta'en, we should have heard the news;
Had he been slain, we should have heard the news;
Or had he 'scap'd, methinks we should have heard
The happy tidings of his good escape.
How fares my brother? why is he so sad?

Ric. I cannot joy, until I be resolv'd
Where our right valiant father is become.   10
I saw him in the battle range about,
And watch'd him how he singled Clifford forth.
Methought he bore him in the thickest troop
As doth a lion in a herd of neat,
Or as a bear encompass'd round with dogs,
Who having pinch'd a few amd made them cry,
The rest stand all aloof, and bark at him.
So far'd our father with his enemies,
So fled his enemies my warlike father:
Methinks, 'tis prize enough to be his son.   20
See how the morning opes her golden gates,
And takes her farewell of the glorious sun!
How well resembles it the prime of youth,
Trimm'd like a younker, prancing to his love!

                    [*Three suns appear in the air*] †

Edw. Dazzle mine eyes, or do I see three suns?
Ric. Three glorious suns, each one a perfect sun,
Not separated with the racking clouds,

28

But sever'd in a pale clear-shining sky.
See, see, they join, embrace, and seem to kiss,
As if they vow'd some league inviolable :   30
Now are they but one lamp, one light, one sun ;
In this the heaven figures some event.

Edw. 'Tis wondrous strange, the like yet never heard of.
I think it cites us, brother, to the field,
That we, the sons of brave Plantagenet,
Each one already blazing by our meeds,
Should notwithstanding join our lights together,
And over-shine the earth, as this the world.
Whate'er it bodes, henceforward will I bear
Upon my target three fair-shining suns.   40

Ric. Nay, bear three daughters : by your leave I speak it,
You love the breeder better than the male.

Enter a Messenger

But what art thou, whose heavy looks foretell
Some dreadful story hanging on thy tongue ?

Mes. Ah, one that was a woful looker-on
Whenas the noble Duke of York was slain,
Your princely father, and my loving lord !

Edw. O, speak no more, for I have heard too much.

Ric. Say how he died, for I will hear it all.

Mes. Environed he was with many foes,   50
And stood against them, as the hope of Troy   †

29

Against the Greeks that would have enter'd Troy.
But Hercules himself must yield to odds;
And many strokes, though with a little axe,
Hews down and fells the hardest-timber'd oak.
By many hands your father was subdued.
But only slaughter'd by the ireful arm
Of unrelenting Clifford, and the queen;
Who crown'd the gracious duke in high despite,
Laugh'd in his face: and when with grief he wept,   60
The ruthless queen gave him, to dry his cheeks,
A napkin, steeped in the harmless blood
Of sweet young Rutland, by rough Clifford slain:
And after many scorns, many foul taunts,
They took his head, and on the gates of York
They set the same, and there it doth remain,
The saddest spectacle that e'er I view'd.

Edw. Sweet Duke of York, our prop to lean upon,
Now thou art gone, we have no staff, no stay.
O Clifford, boisterous Clifford, thou hast slain   70
The flower of Europe for his chivalry,
And treacherously hast thou vanquish'd him,
For hand to hand he would have vanquish'd thee.
Now my soul's palace is become a prison:
Ah, would she break from hence, that this my body
Might in the ground be closed up in rest!

For never henceforth shall I joy again;
Never, O never, shall I see more joy!

Ric. I cannot weep; for all my body's moisture
Scarce serves to quench my furnace-burning heart: 80
Nor can my tongue unload my heart's great burthen,
For selfsame wind that I should speak withal
Is kindling coals that fires all my breast,
And burns me up with flames that tears would quench.
To weep is to make less the depth of grief:
Tears then for babes; blows and revenge for me!
Richard, I bear thy name, I'll venge thy death,
Or die renowned by attempting it.

Edw. His name that valiant duke hath left with thee;
His dukedom and his chair with me is left.   90

Ric. Nay, if thou be that princely eagle's bird,
Show thy descent by gazing 'gainst the sun:
For chair and dukedom, throne and kingdom say,
Either that is thine, or else thou wert not his.

    March.   Enter Warwick, Marquess of Montague,
               and their army

War. How now, fair lords! What fate! what news
    abroad?

Ric. Great Lord of Warwick, if we should recount
Our baleful news, and at each word's deliverance
Stab poniards in our flesh, till all were told,

The words would add more anguish than the wounds.
O valiant lord, the Duke of York is slain !　　　100
Edw. O Warwick, Warwick ! that Plantagenet,
　　Which held thee dearly as his soul's redemption,
　　Is by the stern Lord Clifford done to death.
War. Ten days ago I drown'd these news in tears ;
　　And now, to add more measure to your woes,
　　I come to tell you things sith then befall'n.
　　After the bloody fray at Wakefield fought,
　　Where your brave father breath'd his latest gasp,
　　Tidings, as swiftly as the posts could run,
　　Were brought me of your loss, and his depart.　　110
　　I, then in London, keeper of the king,
　　Muster'd my soldiers, gather'd flocks of friends,
　　[And very well appointed, as I thought,]
　　March'd toward Saint Alban's to intercept the queen,
　　Bearing the king in my behalf along ;
　　For by my scouts I was advertised,
　　That she was coming with a full intent
　　To dash our late decree in parliament,
　　Touching King Henry's oath, and your succession.
　　Short tale to make, we at Saint Alban's met,　　120
　　Our battles join'd, and both sides fiercely fought :
　　But whether 'twas the coldness of the king,
　　Who look'd full gently on his warlike queen,

That robb'd my soldiers of their heated spleen;
Or whether 'twas report of her success,
Or more than common fear of Clifford's rigour,
Who thunders to his captives blood and death,   †
I cannot judge: but, to conclude with truth,
Their weapons like to lightning came and went;
Our soldiers', like the night-owl's lazy flight,   130
Or like an idle thresher with a flail,   †
Fell gently down, as if they struck their friends.
I cheer'd them up with justice of our cause,
With promise of high pay and great rewards:
But all in vain, they had no heart to fight,
And we in them no hope to win the day,
So that we fled; the king unto the queen,
Lord George your brother, Norfolk, and myself,
In haste, post-haste, are come to join with you;
For in the marches here we heard you were,   140
Making another head to fight again.

Edw. Where is the Duke of Norfolk, gentle Warwick?
And when came George from Burgundy to England?

War. Some six miles off the duke is with the soldiers,
And for your brother, he was lately sent
From your kind aunt, Duchess of Burgundy,
With aid of soldiers to this needful war.

Ric. 'Twas odds, belike, when valiant Warwick fled:

Oft have I heard his praises in pursuit,
But ne'er till now his scandal of retire.   150

War. Nor now my scandal, Richard, dost thou hear ;
For thou shalt know this strong right hand of mine
Can pluck the diadem from faint Henry's head,
And wring the awful sceptre from his fist,
Were he as famous, and as bold in war,
As he is fam'd for mildness, peace, and prayer.

Ric. I know it well, Lord Warwick ; blame me not :
'Tis love I bear thy glories makes me speak.
But in this troublous time what 's to be done ?
Shall we go throw away our coats of steel,   160
And wrap our bodies in black mourning gowns,
Numbering our Ave-Maries with our beads ?
Or shall we on the helmets of our foes
Tell our devotion with revengeful arms ?
If for the last, say ay, and to it, lords.

War. Why, therefore Warwick came to seek you out,
And therefore comes my brother Montague.
Attend me, lords.   The proud insulting queen,
With Clifford, and the haught Northumberland,
And of their feather many moe proud birds,   170
Have wrought the easy-melting king, like wax.
He swore consent to your succession,
His oath enrolled in the parliament ;

And now to London all the crew are gone,
To frustrate both his oath and what beside
May make against the house of Lancaster.
Their power, I think, is thirty thousand strong:
Now, if the help of Norfolk, and myself,
With all the friends that thou, brave Earl of March,
Amongst the loving Welshmen canst procure,   180
Will but amount to five and twenty thousand,
Why, Via ! to London will we march [amain,]
And once again bestride our foaming steeds,
And once again cry ' Charge upon our foes ! '
But never once again turn back and fly.

Ric. Ay, now methinks I hear great Warwick speak :
Ne'er may he live to see a sunshine day,
That cries ' Retire,' if Warwick bid him stay.

Edw. Lord Warwick, on thy shoulder will I lean,
And when thou fail'st—as God forbid the hour !—   190
Must Edward fall, which peril heaven forfend !

War. No longer Earl of March, but Duke of York :
The next degree is England's royal throne ;
For King of England shalt thou be proclaim'd
In every borough as we pass along,
And he that throws not up his cap for joy
Shall for the fault make forfeit of his head.
King Edward, valiant Richard, Montague,

Stay we no longer, dreaming of renown,
But sound the trumpets, and about our task. 200

Ric. Then, Clifford, were thy heart as hard as steel,
As thou hast shown it flinty by thy deeds,
I come to pierce it, or to give thee mine.

Edw. Then strike up drums, God and Saint George for us !

Enter a Messenger

War. How now ? what news ?

Mes. The Duke of Norfolk sends you word by me,
The queen is coming with a puissant host ;
And craves your company, for speedy counsel.

War. Why then it sorts, brave warriors, let 's away.

Exeunt

SCENE II

Before York

*Flourish. Enter King Henry, Queen Margaret, the Prince of
Wales, Clifford, and Northumberland, with drum and
trumpets*

Mar. Welcome, my lord, to this brave town of York ;
Yonder 's the head of that arch-enemy
That sought to be encompass'd with your crown :
Doth not the object cheer your heart, my lord ?

36

K.H. Ay, as the rocks cheer them that fear their wreck :
    To see this sight, it irks my very soul.
    Withhold revenge, dear God ! 'tis not my fault,
    Nor wittingly have I infring'd my vow.

Cli. My gracious liege, this too much lenity
    And harmful pity must be laid aside.   10
    To whom do lions cast their gentle looks ?
    Not to the beast that would usurp their den.
    Whose hand is that the forest bear doth lick ?
    Not his that spoils her young before her face.
    Who 'scapes the lurking serpent's mortal sting ?
    Not he that sets his foot upon her back.
    The smallest worm will turn, being trodden on,
    And doves will peck in safeguard of their brood.
    Ambitious York did level at thy crown,
    Thou smiling while he knit his angry brows :   20
    He, but a duke, would have his son a king,
    And raise his issue, like a loving sire ;
    Thou, being a king, blest with a goodly son,
    Didst yield consent to disinherit him,
    Which argued thee a most unloving father.   †
    Unreasonable creatures feed their young,
    And though man's face be fearful to their eyes,
    Yet, in protection of their tender ones,
    Who hath not seen them, even with those wings

Which sometime they have us'd in fearful flight,
Make war with him that climb'd unto their nest,   31
Offering their own lives in their young's defence?
For shame, my liege, make them your precedent!
Were it not pity that this goodly boy
Should lose his birthright by his father's fault,
And long hereafter say unto his child,
'What my great-grandfather and grandsire got
My careless father fondly gave away'?
Ah, what a shame were this! Look on the boy,
And let his manly face, which promiseth   40
Successful fortune, steel thy melting heart
To hold thine own, and leave thine own with him.

K.H. Full well hath Clifford play'd the orator,
Inferring arguments of mighty force.
But, Clifford, tell me, didst thou never hear
That things ill-got had ever bad success?
And happy always was it for that son
Whose father for his hoarding went to hell?
I'll leave my son my virtuous deeds behind,
And would my father had left me no more!   50
For all the rest is held at such a rate
As brings a thousand-fold more care to keep
Than in possession any jot of pleasure.
Ah, cousin York! would thy best friends did know

How it doth grieve me that thy head is here !

*Mar.*My lord, cheer up your spirits : our foes are nigh,
And this soft courage makes your followers faint.
You promised knighthood to our forward son ;
Unsheathe your sword, and dub him presently.
Edward, kneel down.   60

*K.H.*Edward Plantagenet, arise a knight,
And learn this lesson ; draw thy sword in right.

Pri. My gracious father, by your kingly leave,
I'll draw it as apparent to the crown,
And in that quarrel use it to the death.

Cli. Why, that is spoken like a toward prince.

Enter a Messenger

Mes. Royal commanders, be in readiness,
For with a band of thirty thousand men
Comes Warwick, backing of the Duke of York ;
And in the towns, as they do march along,   70
Proclaims him king, and many fly to him :
Darraign your battle, for they are at hand.

Cli. I would your highness would depart the field,
The queen hath best success when you are absent.

*Mar.*Ay, good my lord, and leave us to our fortune.

*K.H.*Why, that's my fortune too, therefore I'll stay.

*Nor.*Be it with resolution then to fight.

Pri. My royal father, cheer these noble lords,

And hearten those that fight in your defence :
Unsheathe your sword, good father ; cry ' Saint
George ! '   80
[*Cli.* Pitch we our battle here for hence we will not move]
    March.   Enter Edward, George, Richard, Warwick,
        Norfolk, Montague, and Soldiers

*Edw.*Now, perjur'd Henry, wilt thou kneel for grace,
And set thy diadem upon my head ?
Or bide the mortal fortune of the field ?

*Mar.*Go, rate thy minions, proud insulting boy !
Becomes it thee to be thus bold in terms
Before thy sovereign and thy lawful king ?

*Edw.*I am his king, and he should bow his knee ;
I was adopted heir by his consent :

Geo. Since when, his oath is broke ; for, as I hear,
You, that are king, though he do wear the crown,   90
Have caus'd him, by new act of parliament,
To blot out me, and put his own son in.

Cli. And reason too,
Who should succeed the father but the son ?

Ric. Are you there, butcher ?   O, I cannot speak !

Cli. Ay, crook-back, here I stand to answer thee,
Or any he the proudest of thy sort.

Ric. 'Twas you that kill'd young Rutland, was it not ?

Cli. Ay, and old York, and yet not satisfied.

Ric. For God's sake, lords, give signal to the fight.   100

War. What say'st thou, Henry, wilt thou yield the crown?

Mar. Why, how now, long-tongu'd Warwick! dare you
       speak?

    When you and I met at Saint Alban's last,

    Your legs did better service than your hands.

War. Then 'twas my turn to fly, and now 'tis thine.

Cli. You said so much before, and yet you fled.

War. 'Twas not your valour, Clifford, drove me thence.

Nor. No, nor your manhood that durst make you stay.

Ric. Northumberland, I hold thee reverently.

    Break off the parley, for scarce I can refrain   110

    The execution of my big-swoln heart

    Upon that Clifford, that cruel child-killer.

Cli. I slew thy father, call'st thou him a child?

Ric. Ay, like a dastard and a treacherous coward,

    As thou didst kill our tender brother Rutland;

    But ere sunset I'll make thee curse the deed.

K.H. Have done with words, my lords, and hear me speak.

Mar. Defy them then, or else hold close thy lips.

K.H. I prithee, give no limits to my tongue:

    I am a king, and privileg'd to speak.   120

Cli. My liege, the wound that bred this meeting here

    Cannot be cur'd by words; therefore be still.

Ric. Then, executioner, unsheathe thy sword:

By Him that made us all, I am resolv'd
That Clifford's manhood lies upon his tongue.

Edw. Say, Henry, shall I have my right, or no?
A thousand men have broke their fasts to-day,
That ne'er shall dine, unless thou yield the crown.

War. If thou deny, their blood upon thy head,
For York in justice puts his armour on.　　　　　130

Pri. If that be right which Warwick says is right,
There is no wrong, but every thing is right.

Ric. Whoever got thee, there thy mother stands;　　†
For, well I wot, thou hast thy mother's tongue.

Mar. But thou art neither like thy sire nor dam,
But like a foul mis-shapen stigmatic,
Mark'd by the destinies to be avoided,
As venom toads, or lizards' dreadful stings.

Ric. Iron of Naples, hid with English gilt,
Whose father bears the title of a king,　　　　　140
(As if a channel should be call'd the sea)
Sham'st thou not, knowing whence thou art extraught,
To let thy tongue detect thy base-born heart?　†

Edw. A wisp of straw were worth a thousand crowns,
To make this shameless callet know herself.
Helen of Greece was fairer far than thou,
Although thy husband may be Menelaus;
And ne'er was Agamemnon's brother wrong'd

By that false woman, as this king by thee.
His father revell'd in the heart of France,   150
And tam'd the king, and made the dauphin stoop ;
And had he match'd according to his state,
He might have kept that glory to this day ;
But when he took a beggar to his bed,
And grac'd thy poor sire with his bridal-day,
Even then that sunshine brew'd a shower for him,
That wash'd his father's fortunes forth of France,
And heap'd sedition on his crown at home.
For what hath broach'd this tumult but thy pride ?
Hadst thou been meek, our title still had slept,   160
And we, in pity of the gentle king,
Had slipp'd our claim until another age.

Geo. But when we saw our sunshine made thy spring,
And that thy summer bred us no increase,
We set the axe to thy usurping root ;
And though the edge hath something hit ourselves,
Yet, know thou, since we have begun to strike,
We'll never leave till we have hewn thee down,
Or bath'd thy growing with our heated bloods.

Edw. And in this resolution, I defy thee,   170
Not willing any longer conference,
Since thou deniest the gentle king to speak.
Sound trumpets ! let our bloody colours wave !

43

And either victory, or else a grave.

*Mar.*Stay, Edward.

*Edw.*No, wrangling woman, we'll no longer stay:
These words will cost ten thousand lives this day.

Exeunt

SCENE III

*A field of battle between Towton and Saxton,
in Yorkshire*

Alarum. Excursions. Enter Warwick

*War.*Forspent with toil, as runners with a race,
I lay me down a little while to breathe;
For strokes receiv'd, and many blows repaid,
Have robb'd my strong-knit sinews of their strength,
And spite of spite needs must I rest awhile.

Enter Edward, runnung

*Edw.*Smile, gentle heaven! or strike, ungentle death!
For this world frowns, and Edward's sun is clouded.

*War.*How now, my lord, what hap? what hope of good?

Enter George

Geo. Our hap is loss, our hope but sad despair;
Our ranks are broke, and ruin follows us:
What counsel give you? whither shall we fly?

10

44

*Edw.*Bootless is flight, they follow us with wings,
　　And weak we are, and cannot shun pursuit.

Enter Richard

Ric. Ah, Warwick, why hast thou withdrawn thyself?
　　Thy brother's blood the thirsty earth hath drunk,
　　Broach'd with the steely point of Clifford's lance;
　　And in the very pangs of death he cried,
　　Like to a dismal clangor heard from far,
　　'Warwick, revenge! brother, revenge my death!'
　　So, underneath the belly of their steeds,　　　　　20
　　That stain'd their fetlocks in his smoking blood,
　　The noble gentleman gave up the ghost.

*War.*Then let the earth be drunken with our blood:
　　I'll kill my horse, because I will not fly.
　　Why stand we like soft-hearted women here,
　　Wailing our losses, whiles the foe doth rage,
　　And look upon, as if the tragedy
　　Were play'd in jest, by counterfeiting actors?
　　Here on my knee I vow to God above,
　　I'll never pause again, never stand still,　　　　　30
　　Till either death hath clos'd these eyes of mine,
　　Or fortune given me measure of revenge.

*Edw.*O Warwick, I do bend my knee with thine,
　　And in this vow do chain my soul to thine!
　　And, ere my knee rise from the earth's cold face,

    I throw my hands, mine eyes, my heart to Thee,
    Thou setter up and plucker down of kings ;
    Beseeching Thee, if with Thy will it stands
    That to my foes this body must be prey,
    Yet that Thy brazen gates of heaven may ope,   **40**
    And give sweet passage to my sinful soul !
    Now, lords, take leave until we meet again,
    Where'er it be, in heaven, or in earth.

Ric. Brother, give me thy hand, and, gentle Warwick,
    Let me embrace thee in my weary arms :
    I, that did never weep, now melt with woe
    That winter should cut off our spring-time so.

War. Away, away ! Once more, sweet lords, farewell.

Geo. Yet let us all together to our troops,
    And give them leave to fly that will not stay ;   **50**
    And call them pillars that will stand to us ;
    And, if we thrive, promise them such rewards
    As victors wear at the Olympian games :
    This may plant courage in their quailing breasts,
    For yet is hope of life and victory.
    Forslow no longer, make we hence amain.   *Exeunt*

SCENE IV   †

Another part of the field

Excursions.   Enter Richard and Clifford

Ric. Now, Clifford, I have singled thee alone :
    Suppose this arm is for the Duke of York,
    And this for Rutland, both bound to revenge,
    Wert thou environ'd with a brazen wall.

Cli. Now, Richard, I am with thee here alone :
    This is the hand that stabb'd thy father York,
    And this the hand that slew thy brother Rutland,
    And here 's the heart that triumphs in their death,
    And cheers these hands, that slew thy sire and brother,
    To execute the like upon thyself ;   10
    And so, have at thee !

            They fight.   Warwick comes ;   Clifford flies

Ric. Nay, Warwick, single out some other chase ;
    For I myself will hunt this wolf to death.   *Exeunt*

SCENE V

Another part of the field

Alarum.   Enter King Henry alone

*K.H.*This battle fares like to the morning's war,
When dying clouds contend with growing light,
What time the shepherd, blowing of his nails,
Can neither call it perfect day nor night.
Now sways it this way, like a mighty sea,
Forc'd by the tide to combat with the wind ;
Now sways it that way, like the selfsame sea,
Forced to retire by fury of the wind :
Sometime the flood prevails, and then the wind ;
Now one the better, then another best ;   10
Both tugging to be victors, breast to breast,
Yet neither conqueror nor conquered :
So is the equal poise of this fell war.
Here on this molehill will I sit me down.
To whom God will, there be the victory !
For Margaret my queen, and Clifford too,
Have chid me from the battle ; swearing both
They prosper best of all when I am thence.
Would I were dead, if God's good will were so !
For what is in this world but grief and woe ?   20

O God! methinks it were a happy life,
To be no better than a homely swain,
To sit upon a hill, as I do now,
To carve out dials quaintly, point by point,
Thereby to see the minutes how they run,
How many make the hour full complete,
How many hours bring about the day,
How many days will finish up the year,
How many years a mortal man may live.
When this is known, then to divide the times: 30
So many hours must I tend my flock;
So many hours must I take my rest;
So many hours must I contemplate;
So many hours must I sport myself;
So many days my ewes have been with young;
So many weeks ere the poor fools will ean;
So many years ere I shall shear the fleece:
So minutes, hours, days, months, and years,
Pass'd over to the end they were created,
Would bring white hairs unto a quiet grave.   40
Ah, what a life were this! how sweet! how lovely!
Gives not the hawthorn-bush a sweeter shade
To shepherds looking on their silly sheep,
Than doth a rich embroider'd canopy
To kings that fear their subjects' treachery?

49

O, yes, it doth ; a thousand-fold it doth.
And to conclude, the shepherd's homely curds,
His cold thin drink out of his leather bottle,
His wonted sleep under a fresh tree's shade,
All which secure and sweetly he enjoys,   50
Is far beyond a prince's delicates,
His viands sparkling in a golden cup,
His body couched in a curious bed,
When care, mistrust, and treason waits on him.

    Alarum.   Enter a Son that has killed his father,
                         dragging in the body

Son. Ill blows the wind that profits nobody.
This man, whom hand to hand I slew in fight,
May be possessed with some store of crowns,
And I, that haply take them from him now,
May yet ere night yield both my life and them
To some man else, as this dead man doth me.   60
Who 's this ?   O God ! it is my father's face,
Whom in this conflict I (unwares) have kill'd.
O heavy times, begetting such events !
From London by the king was I press'd forth ;
My father, being the Earl of Warwick's man,
Come on the part of York, press'd by his master ;
And I, who at his hands receiv'd my life,
Have by my hands of life bereaved him.

Pardon me, God, I knew not what I did !
And pardon, father, for I knew not thee !   70
My tears shall wipe away these bloody marks ;
And no more words till they have flow'd their fill.

K.H. O piteous spectacle !   O bloody times !
Whiles lions war and battle for their dens,
Poor harmless lambs abide their enmity.
Weep, wretched man, I 'll aid thee tear for tear ;
And let our hearts and eyes, like civil war,
Be blind with tears, and break o'ercharg'd with grief.

*Enter a Father that has killed his son, bringing in
the body*

Father. Thou that so stoutly hast resisted me,
Give me thy gold, if thou hast any gold ;   80
For I have bought it with an hundred blows.
But let me see : is this our foeman's face ?
Ah, no, no, no, it is mine only son !
Ah, boy, if any life be left in thee,
Throw up thine eye ! see, see what showers arise,
Blown with the windy tempest of my heart,
Upon thy wounds, that kill mine eye and heart !
O, pity, God, this miserable age !
What stratagems, how fell, how butcherly,
Erroneous, mutinous and unnatural,   90
This deadly quarrel daily doth beget !

O boy, thy father gave thee life too soon,
And hath bereft thee of thy life too late!

K.H. Woe above woe! grief more than common grief!
O that my death would stay these ruthful deeds!
O, pity, pity, gentle heaven, pity!
The red rose and the white are on his face,
The fatal colours of our striving houses:
The one his purple blood right well resembles;
The other his pale cheeks, methinks, presenteth: 100
Wither one rose, and let the other flourish;
If you contend, a thousand lives must wither.

Son. How will my mother, for a father's death,
Take on with me, and ne'er be satisfied!

Father. How will my wife, for slaughter of my son,
Shed seas of tears, and ne'er be satisfied!

K.H. How will the country, for these woful chances,
Misthink the king, and not be satisfied!

Son. Was ever son so rued a father's death?

Father. Was ever father so bemoan'd his son?   110

K.H. Was ever king so griev'd for subjects' woe?
Much is your sorrow; mine ten times so much.

Son. I'll bear thee hence, where I may weep my fill.

                     Exit with the body

Father. These arms of mine shall be thy winding-sheet;
My heart, sweet boy, shall be thy sepulchre,

For from my heart thine image ne'er shall go ;
My sighing breast shall be thy funeral bell ;
And so obsequious will thy father be,
Even for the loss of thee, having no more,
As Priam was for all his valiant sons.   120
I 'll bear thee hence, and let them fight that will,
For I have murdered where I should not kill.

Exit with the body

*K.H.*Sad-hearted men, much overgone with care,
Here sits a king more woful than you are.

*Alarums.   Excursions.   Enter Queen Margaret, the
Prince, and Exeter*

Pri. Fly, father, fly ! for all your friends are fled,
And Warwick rages like a chafed bull :
Away ! for death doth hold us in pursuit.

*Mar.*Mount you, my lord, towards Berwick post amain :
Edward and Richard, like a brace of greyhounds
Having the fearful flying hare in sight,   130
With fiery eyes, sparkling for very wrath,
And bloody steel grasp'd in their ireful hands,
Are at our backs ; and therefore hence amain.

*Exe.*Away ! for vengeance comes along with them :
Nay, stay not to expostulate, make speed,
Or else come after : I 'll away before.

*K.H.*Nay, take me with thee, good sweet Exeter :

53

Not that I fear to stay, but love to go
Whither the queen intends.   Forward, away !

Exeunt

SCENE VI

Another part of the field

A loud alarum.   Enter Clifford, wounded

Cli. Here burns my candle out ; ay, here it dies,
Which, whiles it lasted, gave King Henry light.
O Lancaster, I fear thy overthrow
More than my body's parting with my soul !
My love and fear glued many friends to thee,
And now I fall, thy tough commixture melts,   †
Impairing Henry, strengthening misproud York ;
[The common people swarm like summer flies ;]   †
And whither fly the gnats but to the sun ?
And who shines now but Henry's enemies ?   10
O Phœbus, hadst thou never given consent
That Phaëthon should check thy fiery steeds,
Thy burning car never had scorch'd the earth !
And, Henry, hadst thou sway'd as kings should do,
Or as thy father and his father did,
Giving no ground unto the house of York,

54

{They never then had sprung like summer flies ;}   †
I and ten thousand in this luckless realm
Had left no mourning widows for our death ;
And thou this day hadst kept thy chair in peace.   20
For what doth cherish weeds but gentle air ?
And what makes robbers bold but too much lenity ?
Bootless are plaints, and cureless are my wounds ;
No way to fly, nor strength to hold out flight :
The foe is merciless, and will not pity ;
For at their hands I have deserv'd no pity.
The air hath got into my deadly wounds,
And much effuse of blood doth make me faint.
Come, York and Richard, Warwick, and the rest ;
I stabb'd your father's bosoms, split my breast.   30

He faints

Alarum and retreat.   Enter Edward, George, Richard,
Montague, Warwick, and Soldiers

Edw. Now breathe we, lords : good fortune bids us pause,
And smooth the frowns of war with peaceful looks.
Some troops pursue the bloody-minded queen,
That led calm Henry, though he were a king,
As doth a sail, fill'd with a fretting gust,
Command an argosy to stem the waves.
But think you, lords, that Clifford fled with them ?
War. No, 'tis impossible he should escape ;

For, though before his face I speak the words,
Your brother Richard mark'd him for the grave :   **40**
And wheresoe'er he is, he 's surely dead.

Clifford groans, and dies

Edw. Whose soul is that which takes her heavy leave ?

Ric. A deadly groan, like life and death's departing.

Edw. See who it is : and, now the battle 's ended,
If friend or foe, let him be gently used.

Ric. Revoke that doom of mercy, for 'tis Clifford,
Who not contented that he lopp'd the branch,
In hewing Rutland, when his leaves put forth,
But set his murdering knife unto the root,
From whence that tender spray did sweetly spring,   **50**
I mean our princely father, Duke of York.

War. From off the gates of York fetch down the head,
Your father's head, which Clifford placed there ;
Instead whereof let this supply the room :
Measure for measure must be answered.

Edw. Bring forth that fatal screech-owl to our house,
That nothing sung but death to us and ours :
Now death shall stop his dismal threatening sound,
And his ill-boding tongue no more shall speak.

War. I think his understanding is bereft.   **60**
Speak, Clifford, dost thou know who speaks to thee ?
Dark cloudy death o'ershades his beams of life,

And he nor sees, nor hears us what we say.

Ric. O, would he did ! and so perhaps he doth :
'Tis but his policy to counterfeit,
Because he would avoid such bitter taunts
Which in the time of death he gave our father.

Geo. If so thou think'st, vex him with eager words.

Ric. Clifford, ask mercy and obtain no grace.

Edw. Clifford, repent in bootless penitence.   70

War. Clifford, devise excuses for thy faults.

Geo. While we devise fell tortures for thy faults.

Ric. Thou didst love York, and I am son to York.

Edw. Thou pitied'st Rutland, I will pity thee.

Geo. Where's Captain Margaret, to fence you now ?

War. They mock thee, Clifford : swear as thou wast wont.

Ric. What, not an oath ? nay, then the world goes hard,
When Clifford cannot spare his friends an oath.
I know by that he's dead, and, by my soul,
If this right hand would buy two hours' life,   80
That I in all despite might rail at him,
This hand should chop it off, and with the issuing   †
    blood
Stifle the villian, whose unstaunched thirst
York and young Rutland could not satisfy.

War. Ay, but he's dead : off with the traitor's head,
And rear it in the place your father's stands.

And now to London with triumphant march,
There to be crowned England's royal king :
From whence shall Warwick cut the sea to France,
And ask the Lady Bona for thy queen :   90
So shalt thou sinew both these lands together,
And, having France thy friend, thou shalt not dread
The scatter'd foe that hopes to rise again ;
For though they cannot greatly sting to hurt,
Yet look to have them buzz to offend thine ears.
First will I see the coronation,
And then to Brittany I'll cross the sea,
To effect this marriage, so it please my lord.

Edw. Even as thou wilt, sweet Warwick, let it be ;
For in thy shoulder do I build my seat ;   100
And never will I undertake the thing
Wherein thy counsel and consent is wanting.
Richard, I will create thee Duke of Gloucester,
And George, of Clarence : Warwick, as ourself,
Shall do and undo as him pleaseth best.

Ric. Let me be Duke of Clarence, George of Gloucester ;
For Gloucester's dukedom is too ominous.

War. Tut, that's a foolish observation :
Richard, be Duke of Gloucester. Now to London,
To see these honours in possession. *Exeunt* 110

Act Third

SCENE I

A forest in the north of England

Enter two Keepers, with cross-bows in their hands †

1.K. Under this thick-grown brake we 'll shroud our-
    selves ;
    For through this laund anon the deer will come,
    And in this covert will we make our stand,
    Culling the principal of all the deer.
2.K. I 'll stay above the hill, so both may shoot.
1.K. That cannot be ; the noise of thy cross-bow
    Will scare the herd, and so my shoot is lost.
    Here stand we both, and aim we at the best :
    And, for the time shall not seem tedious,
    I 'll tell thee what befel me on a day   10
    In this self-place, where now we mean to stand.
2.K. Here comes a man, let 's stay till he be past.

    Enter King Henry, [disguised,] with a prayer-book

K.H. From Scotland am I stol'n, even of pure love.
    To greet mine own land with my wishful sight.
    No, Harry, Harry, 'tis no land of thine ;

    Thy place is fill'd, thy sceptre wrung from thee,
    Thy balm wash'd off, wherewith thou wast anointed:
    No bending knee will call thee Cæsar now,
    No humble suitors press to speak for right,
    No, not a man comes for redress of thee;   20
    For how can I help them, and not myself?

1.K. Ay, here's a deer whose skin's a keeper's fee:
    This is the quondam king; let's seize upon him.

K.H. Let me embrace thee, sour adversity,   †
    For wise men say it is the wisest course.

2.K. Why linger we? let us lay hands upon him.

1.K. Forbear awhile, we'll hear a little more.

K.H. My queen and son are gone to France for aid;
    And, as I hear, the great commanding Warwick
    Is thither gone, to crave the French king's sister   30
    To wife for Edward: if this news be true,
    Poor queen and son, your labour is but lost;
    For Warwick is a subtle orator,
    And Lewis a prince soon won with moving words.
    By this account then Margaret may win him;
    For she's a woman to be pitied much:
    Her sighs will make a battery in his breast,
    Her tears will pierce into a marble heart;
    The tiger will be mild, whiles she doth mourn;
    And Nero will be tainted with remorse,   40

To hear and see her plaints, her brinish tears.
Aye, but she's come to beg, Warwick to give;
She, on his left side, craving aid for Henry,
He, on his right, asking a wife for Edward.
She weeps, and says, her Henry is depos'd;
He smiles, and says, his Edward is install'd;
That she, poor wretch, for grief can speak no more;
Whiles Warwick tells his title, smooths the wrong,
Inferreth arguments of mighty strength,
And in conclusion wins the king from her,   50
With promise of his sister, and what else,
To strengthen and support King Edward's place.
O Margaret, thus 'twill be, and thou, poor soul,
Art then forsaken, as thou went'st forlorn!

2.K. Say, what art thou that talk'st of kings and queens?

K.H. More than I seem, and less than I was born to:
A man at least, for less I should not be;
And men may talk of kings, and why not I?

2.K. Ay, but thou talk'st as if thou wert a king.

K.H. Why, so I am, in mind; and that's enough.   60

2.K. But if thou be a king, where is thy crown?

K.H. My crown is in my heart, not on my head;
Not deck'd with diamonds, and Indian stones;
Nor to be seen: my crown is call'd content;
A crown it is that seldom kings enjoy.

2.K. Well, if you be a king crown'd with content,
    Your crown content, and you, must be contented
    To go along with us ; for, as we think,
    You are the king King Edward hath depos'd ;
    And we his subjects, sworn in all allegiance,   70
    Will apprehend you as his enemy.

K.H. But did you never swear, and break an oath.

2.K. No, never such an oath, nor will not now.

K.H. Where did you dwell, when I was King of England ?

2.K. Here in this country, where we now remain.

K.H. I was anointed king at nine months old ;
    My father and my grandfather were kings ;
    And you were sworn true subjects unto me :
    And tell me, then, have you not broke your oaths ?

1.K. No ;   80
    For we were subjects but while you were king.

K.H. Why, am I dead ? do I not breathe a man ?
    Ah, simple men, you know not what you swear !
    Look, as I blow this feather from my face,
    And as the air blows it to me again,
    Obeying with my wind when I do blow,
    And yielding to another when it blows,
    Commanded always by the greater gust ;
    Such is the lightness of you common men.
    But do not break your oaths, for of that sin   90

My mild entreaty shall not make you guilty.
Go where you will, the king shall be commanded,
And be you kings, command, and I'll obey.

1.*K.* We are true subjects to the king, King Edward.

K.H. So would you be again to Henry,
If he were seated as King Edward is.

1.*K.* We charge you, in God's name, and the king's,
To go with us unto the officers.

K.H. In God's name, lead, your king's name be obey'd,
And what God will, that let your king perform,   100
And what he will, I humbly yield unto.   *Exeunt*

SCENE II

London.   The palace

Enter King Edward, Gloucester, Clarence, and Lady Grey

K.E. Brother of Gloucester, at Saint Alban's field
This lady's husband, Sir Richard Grey, was slain,
His land then seiz'd on by the conqueror:
Her suit is now to repossess those lands,
Which we in justice cannot well deny,
Because in quarrel of the house of York
The worthy gentleman did lose his life.

Glo. Your highness shall do well to grant her suit;

It were dishonour to deny it her.

*K.E.*It were no less, but yet I'll make a pause.   10

Glo. (*aside to Cla.*) Yea, is it so?
I see the lady hath a thing to grant,
Before the king will grant her humble suit.

Cla. (*aside to Glo.*) He knows the game: how true he keeps
the wind!

Glo. (*aside to Cla.*) Silence!

*K.E.*Widow, we will consider of your suit,
And come some other time to know our mind.

*L.G.*Right gracious lord, I cannot brook delay:
May it please your highness to resolve me now,
And what your pleasure is, shall satisfy me.   20

Glo. (*aside to Cla.*) Ay, widow? then I'll warrant you
all your lands,
An if what pleases him shall pleasure you.
Fight closer, or, good faith, you'll catch a blow.

Cla. (*aside to Glo.*) I fear her not, unless she chance to fall.

Glo. (*aside to Cla.*) God forbid that! for he'll take
vantages.

*K.E.*How many children hast thou, widow? tell me.

Cla. (*aside to Glo.*) I think he means to beg a child of her.

Glo. (*aside to Cla.*) Nay, then whip me: he'll rather give
her two.

*L.G.*Three, my most gracious lord.

Glo. (*aside to Cla.*) You shall have four, if you 'll be rul'd
        by him.   30

K.E.'Twere pity they should lose their father's lands.

*L.G.*Be pitiful, dread lord, and grant it then.

*K.E.*Lords, give us leave : I 'll try this widow's wit.

Glo. (*aside to Cla.*) Ay, good leave have you, for you will
        have leave,

    Till youth take leave, and leave you to the crutch.

                        Gloucester and Clarence retire

*K.E.*Now tell me, madam, do you love your children ?

*L.G.*Ay, full as dearly as I love myself.

*K.E.*And would you not do much to do them good ?

*L.G.*To do them good, I would sustain some harm.

*K.E.*Then get your husband's lands, to do them good.   40

*L.G.*Therefore I came unto your majesty.

*K.E.*I 'll tell you how these lands are to be got.

*L.G.*So shall you bind me to your highness' service.

*K.E.*What service wilt thou do me, if I give them ?

*L.G.*What you command, that rests in me to do.

*K.E.*But you will take exceptions to my boon.

*L.G.*No, gracious lord, except I cannot do it.

*K.E.*Ay, but thou canst do what I mean to ask.

*L.G.*Why, then I will do what your grace commands.

Glo. (*aside to Cla.*) He plies her hard, and much rain wears
        the marble.   50

Cla. (*aside to Glo.*) As red as fire ! nay, then her wax must melt.

L.G. Why stops my lord ? shall I not hear my task ?

K.E. An easy task, 'tis but to love a king.

L.G. That 's soon perform'd, because I am a subject.

K.E. Why, then, thy husband's lands I freely give thee.

L.G. I take my leave with many thousand thanks.

Glo. (*aside to Clar.*) The match is made, she seals it with a curt'sy.

K.E. But stay thee, 'tis the fruits of love I mean.

L.G. The fruits of love I mean, my loving liege.

K.E. Ay, but, I fear me, in another sense.   60

    What love, think'st thou, I sue so much to get ?

L.G. My love till death, my humble thanks, my prayers,

    That love which virtue begs and virtue grants.

K.E. No, by my troth, I did not mean such love.

L.G. Why then, you mean not as I thought you did.

K.E. But now you partly may perceive my mind.

L.G. My mind will never grant what I perceive

    Your highness aims at, if I aim aright.

K.E. To tell thee plain, I aim to lie with thee.

L.G. To tell you plain, I had rather lie in prison.   70

K.E. Why, then thou shalt not have thy husband's lands.

L.G. Why, then mine honesty shall be my dower,

    For by that loss I will not purchase them.

K.E. Therein thou wrong'st thy children mightily.

L.G. Herein your highness wrongs both them and me.
But, mighty lord, this merry inclination
Accords not with the sadness of my suit :
Please you dismiss me, either with ' ay ' or ' no.'

K.E. ' Ay,' if thou wilt say ' ay ' to my request ;
' No,' if thou dost say ' no ' to my demand.   80

L.G. Then ' no,' my lord : my suit is at an end.

Glo. (*aside to Cla.*) The widow likes him not, she knits
her brows.

Cla. (*aside to Glo.*) He is the bluntest wooer in Christen-
dom.

K.E. (*aside*) Her looks doth argue her replete with modesty,
Her words do show her wit incomparable,
All her perfections challenge sovereignty ;
One way or other, she is for a king,
And she shall be my love, or else my queen.—
Say that King Edward take thee for his queen ?

L.G. 'Tis better said than done, my gracious lord :   90
I am a subject fit to jest withal,
But far unfit to be a sovereign.

K.E. Sweet widow, by my state I swear to thee,
I speak no more than what my soul intends,
And that is, to enjoy thee for my love.

L.G. And that is more than I will yield unto :

I know I am too mean to be your queen,
And yet too good to be your concubine.

K.E. You cavil, widow : I did mean, my queen.

L.G. 'Twill grieve your grace my sons should call you
father. 100

K.E. No more than when my daughters call thee mother.
Thou art a widow, and thou hast some children ;
And, by God's mother, I, being but a bachelor,
Have other some : why, 'tis a happy thing
To be the father unto many sons.
Answer no more, for thou shalt be my queen.

Glo. (*aside to Cla.*) The ghostly father now hath done his
shrift.

Cla. (*aside to Glo.*) When he was made a shriver, 'twas for
shift.

K.E. Brothers, you muse what chat we two have had.

Glo. The widow likes it not, for she looks very sad. 110

K.E. You 'ld think it strange if I should marry her.

Cla. To whom, my lord ?

K.E.   Why, Clarence, to myself.

Glo. That would be ten days' wonder at the least.

Cla. That 's a day longer than a wonder lasts.

Glo. By so much is the wonder in extremes.

K.E. Well, jest on, brothers : I can tell you both,
Her suit is granted for her husband's lands.

68

Enter a Nobleman

Nobl. My gracious lord, Henry your foe is taken,
    And brought your prisoner to your palace gate.

K.E. See that he be convey'd unto the Tower: 120
    And go we, brothers, to the man that took him,
    To question of his apprehension.
    Widow, go you along.   Lords, use her honourably.

                      Exeunt all but Gloucester

Glo. Ay, Edward will use women honourably!
    Would he were wasted, marrow, bones, and all,
    That from his loins no hopeful branch may spring,
    To cross me from the golden time I look for!
    And yet, between my soul's desire and me—
    The lustful Edward's title buried—
    Is Clarence, Henry, and his son young Edward,   130
    And all the unlook'd for issue of their bodies,
    To take their rooms, ere I can place myself:
    A cold premeditation for my purpose!
    Why, then, I do but dream on sovereignty;
    Like one that stands upon a promontory,
    And spies a far-off shore, where he would tread,
    Wishing his foot were equal with his eye,
    And chides the sea, that sunders him from thence,
    Saying, he'll lade it dry, to have his way:
    So do I wish the crown, being so far off,   140

And so I chide the means that keeps me from it,
And so I say, I'll cut the causes off,
Flattering me with impossibilities.
My eye's too quick, my heart o'erweens too much,
Unless my hand and strength could equal them.
Well, say there is no kingdom then for Richard;
What other pleasure can the world afford?
I'll make my heaven in a lady's lap,
And deck my body in gay ornaments,
And witch sweet ladies with my words and looks. **150**
O miserable thought! and more unlikely
Than to accomplish twenty golden crowns!
Why, love forswore me in my mother's womb:
And, for I should not deal in her soft laws,
She did corrupt frail nature with some bribe,
To shrink mine arm up like a wither'd shrub; †
To make an envious mountain on my back,
Where sits deformity to mock my body;
To shape my legs of an unequal size,
To disproportion me in every part, **160**
Like to a chaos, or an unlick'd bear-whelp,
That carries no impression like the dam.
And am I then a man to be belov'd?
O monstrous fault, to harbour such a thought!
Then, since this earth affords no joy to me,

70

But to command, to check, to o'erbear such
As are of better person than myself,
I'll make my heaven to dream upon the crown,
And, whiles I live, to account this world but hell,
Until my mis-shap'd trunk, that bears this head,   170
Be round impaled with a glorious crown.
And yet I know not how to get the crown,
For many lives stand between me and home :
And I,—like one lost in a thorny wood,
That rends the thorns and is rent with the thorns,
Seeking a way, and straying from the way,
Not knowing how to find the open air,
But toiling desperately to find it out,—
Torment myself to catch the English crown :
And from that torment I will free myself,   180
Or hew my way out with a bloody axe.
Why, I can smile, and murder whiles I smile,
And cry ' Content ' to that which grieves my heart,
And wet my cheeks with artificial tears,
And frame my face to all occasions.
I'll drown more sailors than the mermaid shall,
I'll slay more gazers than the basilisk,
I'll play the orator as well as Nestor,   †
Deceive more slily than Ulysses could,
And, like a Sinon, take another Troy.   † 190

I can add colours to the chameleon,
Change shapes with Proteus, for advantages,
And set the murderous Machiavel to school.
Can I do this, and cannot get a crown ?
Tut, were it further off, I 'll pluck it down.   *Exit*

† †

SCENE III

France.   The King's palace

Flourish.   Enter Lewis the French King, his sister Bona, his
Admiral, called Bourbon: Prince Edward, Queen Margaret,
and the Earl of Oxford.   Lewis sits, and riseth up again

Lew. Fair Queen of England, worthy Margaret,
Sit down with us : it ill befits thy state,
And birth, that thou shouldst stand while Lewis doth
    sit.
Mar. No, mighty King of France : now Margaret
Must strike her sail, and learn a while to serve,
Where kings command.   I was, I must confess,
Great Albion's queen in former golden days :
But now mischance hath trod my title down,
And with dishonour laid me on the ground ;
Where I must take like seat unto my fortune,   10
And to my humble seat conform myself.

Lew. Why, say, fair queen, whence springs this deep
    despair ?
Mar. From such a cause as fills mine eyes with tears,
    And stops my tongue, while heart is drown'd in cares.
Lew. Whate'er it be, be thou still like thyself,
    And sit thee by our side : (*seats her by him*) yield not
      thy neck
    To fortune's yoke, but let thy dauntless mind
    Still ride in triumph over all mischance.
    Be plain, Queen Margaret, and tell thy grief ;
    It shall be eas'd, if France can yield relief.   20
Mar. Those gracious words revive my drooping thoughts,
    And give my tongue-tied sorrows leave to speak.
    Now, therefore, be it known to noble Lewis,
    That Henry, sole possessor of my love,
    Is, of a king, become a banish'd man,
    And forc'd to live in Scotland a forlorn ;
    While proud ambitious Edward, Duke of York,
    Usurps the regal title, and the seat
    Of England's true anointed lawful king.
    This is the cause that I, poor Margaret,   30
    With this my son, Prince Edward, Henry's heir,
    Am come to crave thy just and lawful aid ;
    And if thou fail us, all our hope is done :
    Scotland hath will to help, but cannot help;

Our people, and our peers, are both misled,
Our treasure seiz'd, our soldiers put to flight,
And, as thou seest, ourselves in heavy plight.

Lew. Renowned queen, with patience calm the storm,
While we bethink a means to break it off.

Mar. The more we stay, the stronger grows our foe. 40

Lew. The more I stay, the more I 'll succour thee.

Mar. O, but impatience waiteth on true sorrow.
And see where comes the breeder of my sorrow !

Enter Warwick

Lew. What 's he approacheth boldly to our presence ?

Mar. Our Earl of Warwick, Edward's greatest friend.

Lew. Welcome, brave Warwick ! What brings thee to
France ?   *He descends.   She ariseth*

Mar. Ay, now begins a second storm to rise,
For this is he that moves both wind and tide.

War. From worthy Edward, king of Albion,
My lord and sovereign, and thy vowed friend, 50
I come, in kindness and unfeigned love,
First, to do greetings to thy royal person,
And then to crave a league of amity ;
And lastly, to confirm that amity
With nuptial knot, if thou vouchsafe to grant
That virtuous Lady Bona, thy fair sister,
To England's king in lawful marriage.

74

Mar.(aside) If that go forward, Henry's hope is done.

War.(to Bona) And, gracious madam, in our king's behalf,

 I am commanded, with your leave and favour,   60

 Humbly to kiss your hand, and with my tongue

 To tell the passion of my sovereign's heart ;

 Where fame, late entering at his heedful ears,

 Hath plac'd thy beauty's image, and thy virtue.

Mar. King Lewis, and Lady Bona, hear me speak,

 Before you answer Warwick.   His demand

 Springs not from Edward's well-meant honest love,

 But from deceit, bred by necessity ;

 For how can tyrants safely govern home,

 Unless abroad they purchase great alliance ?   70

 To prove him tyrant this reason may suffice,

 That Henry liveth still ; but were he dead,

 Yet here Prince Edward stands, King Henry's son.

 Look, therefore, Lewis, that by this league and marriage

 Thou draw not on thy danger, and dishonour ;

 For though usurpers sway the rule a while,

 Yet heavens are just, and time suppresseth wrongs.

War. Injurious Margaret !

Pri.   And why not queen ?

War. Because thy father Henry did usurp,

75

And thou no more art prince than she is queen. 80

Oxf. Then Warwick disannuls great John of Gaunt,
Which did subdue the greatest part of Spain ;
And, after John of Gaunt, Henry the Fourth,
Whose wisdom was a mirror to the wisest ;
And, after that wise prince, Henry the Fifth,
Who by his prowess conquered all France :
From these our Henry lineally descends.

War. Oxford, how haps it, in this smooth discourse,
You told not how Henry the Sixth hath lost
All that which Henry the Fifth had gotten ? 90
Methinks these peers of France should smile at that.
But for the rest, you tell a pedigree
Of threescore and two years, a silly time
To make prescription for a kingdom's worth.

Oxf. Why, Warwick, canst thou speak against thy liege,
Whom thou obeyed'st thirty and six years,
And not bewray thy treason with a blush ?

War. Can Oxford, that did ever fence the right,
Now buckler falsehood with a pedigree ?
For shame leave Henry, and call Edward king. 100

Oxf. Call him my king by whose injurious doom
My elder brother, the Lord Aubrey Vere,
Was done to death ? and more than so, my father,
Even in the downfall of his mellow'd years,

76

When nature brought him to the door of death?
No, Warwick, no; while life upholds this arm,
This arm upholds the house of Lancaster.

*War.*And I the house of York.

*Lew.*Queen Margaret, Prince Edward, and Oxford,
Vouchsafe, at our request, to stand aside,   110
While I use further conference with Warwick.

They stand aloof

*Mar.*Heavens grant that Warwick's words bewitch him
not!

*Lew.*Now, Warwick, tell me, even upon thy conscience,
Is Edward your true king? for I were loath
To link with him that were not lawful chosen.

*War.*Thereon I pawn my credit and mine honour.

*Lew.*But is he gracious in the people's eye?

*War.*The more that Henry was unfortunate.

*Lew.*Then further; all dissembling set aside,
Tell me for truth the measure of his love   120
Unto our sister Bona.

War.   Such it seems
As may beseem a monarch like himself.
Myself have often heard him say, and swear,
That this his love was an eternal plant,
Whereof the root was fix'd in virtue's ground,
The leaves and fruit maintain'd with beauty's sun,

77

Exempt from envy, but not from disdain,   †
Unless the Lady Bona quit his pain.

Lew. Now, sister, let us hear your firm resolve.

Bona. Your grant, or your denial, shall be mine :   130
(*to War.*) Yet I confess that often ere this day,
When I have heard your king's desert recounted,
Mine ear hath tempted judgement to desire.

Lew. Then, Warwick, thus : our sister shall be Edward's ;
And now forthwith shall articles be drawn,
Touching the jointure that your king must make,
Which with her dowry shall be counterpois'd.
Draw near, Queen Margaret, and be a witness
That Bona shall be wife to the English king.

Pri. To Edward, but not to the English king.   140

Mar. Deceitful Warwick ! it was thy device
By this alliance to make void my suit :
Before thy coming Lewis was Henry's friend.

Lew. And still is friend to him and Margaret :
But if your title to the crown be weak,
As may appear by Edward's good success,
Then 'tis but reason that I be releas'd
From giving aid, which late I promised.
Yet shall you have all kindness at my hand
That your estate requires, and mine can yield.   150

War. Henry now lives in Scotland, at his ease ;

78

Where having nothing, nothing can he lose.
And as for you yourself, our quondam queen,
You have a father able to maintain you ;
And better 'twere you troubled him than France.

Mar. Peace, impudent and shameless Warwick, peace,
Proud setter up and puller down of kings !
I will not hence, till, with my talk and tears,
Both full of truth, I make King Lewis behold
Thy sly conveyance, and thy lord's false love,   160
For both of you are birds of selfsame feather.

Post blows a horn within

Lew. Warwick, this is some post to us or thee.

Enter a Post

Post. (*to War.*) My lord ambassador, these letters are for
    you,
Sent from your brother, Marquess Montague :
(*to Lew.*) These from our king, unto your majesty :
(*to Mar.*) And, madam, these for you ; from whom
    I know not.   *They all read their letters*

Oxf. I like it well that our fair queen and mistress
Smiles at her news, while Warwick frowns at his.

Pri. Nay, mark how Lewis stamps, as he were nettled :
I hope all 's for the best.   170

Lew. Warwick, what are thy news ? and yours, fair queen ?

Mar. Mine such as fill my heart with unhop'd joys.

*War.*Mine full of sorrow and heart's discontent.

Lew. What? has your king married the Lady Grey?
    And now, to soothe your forgery and his,
    Sends me a paper to persuade me patience?
    Is this the alliance that he seeks with France?
    Dare he presume to scorn us in this manner?

*Mar.*I told your majesty as much before:
    This proveth Edward's love, and Warwick's honesty. **180**

*War.*King Lewis, I here protest in sight of heaven,
    And by the hope I have of heavenly bliss,
    That I am clear from this misdeed of Edward's;
    No more my king, for he dishonours me,
    But most himself, if he could see his shame.
    Did I forget that by the house of York
    My father came untimely to his death?
    Did I let pass the abuse done to my niece?
    Did I impale him with the regal crown?
    Did I put Henry from his native right?   **190**
    And am I guerdon'd at the last with shame?
    Shame on himself! for my desert is honour:
    And to repair my honour lost for him,
    I here renounce him, and return to Henry.
    My noble queen, let former grudges pass,
    And henceforth I am thy true servitor:
    I will revenge his wrong to Lady Bona,

And replant Henry in his former state.

Mar. Warwick, these words have turn'd my hate to love,
And I forgive, and quite forget old faults,   200
And joy that thou becom'st King Henry's friend.

War. So much his friend, ay, his unfeigned friend,
That, if King Lewis vouchsafe to furnish us
With some few bands of chosen soldiers,
I 'll undertake to land them on our coast,
And force the tyrant from his seat by war.
'Tis not his new-made bride shall succour him :
And as for Clarence, as my letters tell me,
He 's very likely now to fall from him,
For matching more for wanton lust than honour,   210
Or than for strength and safety of our country.

Bona. Dear brother, how shall Bona be reveng'd
But by thy help to this distressed queen ?

Mar. Renowned prince, how shall poor Henry live,
Unless thou rescue him from foul despair ?

Bona. My quarrel, and this English queen's, are one.

War. And mine, fair Lady Bona, joins with yours.

Lew. And mine with hers, and thine, and Margaret's.
Therefore at last I firmly am resolv'd
You shall have aid.   220

Mar. Let me give humble thanks for all at once.

Lew. Then, England's messenger, return in post,

And tell false Edward, thy supposed king,
That Lewis of France is sending over masquers,
To revel it with him, and his new bride :
Thou seest what's past, go fear thy king withal.

Bona. Tell him, in hope he'll prove a widower shortly,
I'll wear the willow garland for his sake.

Mar. Tell him, my mourning weeds are laid aside,
And I am ready to put armour on.   230

War. Tell him from me that he hath done me wrong,
And therefore I'll uncrown him, ere't be long.
There's thy reward, be gone.   *Exit Post*

Lew.   But, Warwick,
Thou and Oxford, with five thousand men,
Shall cross the seas, and bid false Edward battle ;
And, as occasion serves, this noble queen
And prince shall follow with a fresh supply.
Yet, ere thou go, but answer me one doubt,
What pledge have we of thy firm loyalty ?

War. This shall assure my constant loyalty,   240
That if our queen and this young prince agree,
I'll join mine eldest daughter and my joy
To him forthwith in holy wedlock bands.

Mar. Yes, I agree, and thank you for your motion.
Son Edward, she is fair and virtuous,
Therefore delay not, give thy hand to Warwick,

And, with thy hand, thy faith irrevocable,
That only Warwick's daughter shall be thine.

Pri. Yes, I accept her, for she well deserves it ;
And here, to pledge my vow, I give my hand.   250

He gives his hand to Warwick

Lew. Why stay we now ?   These soldiers shall be levied,
And thou, Lord Bourbon, our high admiral,
Shalt waft them over with our royal fleet.
I long till Edward fall by war's mischance,
For mocking marriage with a dame of France.

Exeunt all but Warwick

War. I came from Edward as ambassador,
But I return his sworn and mortal foe :
Matter of marriage was the charge he gave me,
But dreadful war shall answer his demand.
Had he none else to make a stale but me ?   260
Then none but I shall turn his jest to sorrow.
I was the chief that rais'd him to the crown,
And I 'll be chief to bring him down again :
Not that I pity Henry's misery,
But seek revenge on Edward's mockery.   *Exit*

Act Fourth

SCENE I

London.   The palace

Enter Gloucester, Clarence, Somerset, and Montague

Glo. Now tell me, brother Clarence, what think you
    Of this new marriage with the Lady Grey?
    Hath not our brother made a worthy choice?

Cla. Alas, you know, 'tis far from hence to France;
    How could he stay till Warwick made return?

Som. My lords, forbear this talk; here comes the king.

Glo. And his well-chosen bride.

Cla. I mind to tell him plainly what I think.
    *Flourish.   Enter King Edward, attended; Lady Grey, as
       Queen; Pembroke, Stafford, Hastings, and others*

K.E. Now, brother of Clarence, how like you our choice,
    That you stand pensive, as half malcontent?   10

Cla. As well as Lewis of France, or the Earl of Warwick,
    Which are so weak of courage and in judgement
    That they'll take no offence at our abuse.

K.E. Suppose they take offence without a cause,
    They are but Lewis and Warwick: I am Edward,

Your king and Warwick's, and must have my will.

Glo. And shall have your will, because our king :
Yet hasty marriage seldom proveth well.

K.E. Yea, brother Richard, are you offended too ?

Glo. Not I :   20
No, God forbid that I should wish them sever'd
Whom God hath join'd together ; ay, and 'twere pity
To sunder them that yoke so well together.

K.E Setting your scorns and your mislike aside,
Tell me some reason why the Lady Grey
Should not become my wife, and England's queen.
And you too, Somerset and Montague,
Speak freely what you think.

Cla. Then this is mine opinion : that King Lewis
Becomes your enemy, for mocking him   30
About the marriage of the Lady Bona.

Glo. And Warwick, doing what you gave in charge,
Is now dishonoured by this new marriage.

K.E. What if both Lewis and Warwick be appeas'd
By such invention as I can devise ?

Mon. Yet, to have join'd with France in such alliance
Would more have strengthen'd this our common-
        wealth
'Gainst foreign storms than any home-bred marriage.

Has. Why, knows not Montague that of itself

85

England is safe, if true within itself ?   **40**

Mon. But the safer when 'tis back'd with France.

Has. 'Tis better using France than trusting France :
Let us be back'd with God, and with the seas,
Which He hath given for fence impregnable,
And with their helps only defend ourselves ;
In them, and in ourselves, our safety lies.

Cla. For this one speech Lord Hastings well deserves
To have the heir of the Lord Hungerford.

K.E. Ay, what of that ? it was my will and grant ;
And for this once my will shall stand for law.   **50**

Glo. And yet methinks your grace hath not done well,
To give the heir and daughter of Lord Scales
Unto the brother of your loving bride ;
She better would have fitted me or Clarence :
But in your bride you bury brotherhood.

Cla. Or else you would not have bestow'd the heir
Of the Lord Bonville on your new wife's son,
And leave your brothers to go speed elsewhere.

K.E. Alas, poor Clarence ! is it for a wife
That thou art malcontent ? I will provide thee.   **60**

Cla. In choosing for yourself, you show'd your judgement,
Which being shallow, you shall give me leave
To play the broker in mine own behalf ;
And to that end I shortly mind to leave you.

*K.E.*Leave me, or tarry, Edward will be king,
 And not be tied unto his brother's will.

*Q.E.*My lords, before it pleas'd his majesty
 To raise my state to title of a queen,
 Do me but right, and you must all confess
 That I was not ignoble of descent,   70
 And meaner than myself have had like fortune.
 But as this title honours me and mine,
 So your dislike, to whom I would be pleasing,
 Doth cloud my joys with danger and with sorrow.

*K.E.*My love, forbear to fawn upon their frowns :
 What danger or what sorrow can befall thee,
 So long as Edward is thy constant friend,
 And their true sovereign, whom they must obey ?
 Nay, whom they shall obey, and love thee too,
 Unless they seek for hatred at my hands ; 80
 Which if they do, yet will I keep thee safe,
 And they shall feel the vengeance of my wrath.

Glo. I hear, yet say not much, but think the more. *Aside*

Enter a Post

*K.E.*Now, messenger, what letters, or what news
 From France ?

*Post.*My sovereign liege, no letters, and few words,
 But such as I, without your special pardon,
 Dare not relate.

87

K.E. Go to, we pardon thee : therefore, in brief,
    Tell me their words as near as thou canst guess them.   90
    What answer makes King Lewis unto our letters ?

Post. At my depart, these were his very words :
    ' Go tell false Edward, thy supposed king,
    That Lewis of France is sending over masquers
    To revel it with him, and his new bride.'

K.E. Is Lewis so brave ? belike he thinks me Henry.
    But what said Lady Bona to my marriage ?

Post. These were her words, utter'd with mild disdain :
    ' Tell him, in hope he 'll prove a widower shortly,
    I 'll wear the willow garland for his sake.'   100

K.E. I blame not her ; she could say little less ;
    She had the wrong.   But what said Henry's queen ?
    For I have heard that she was there in place.

Post. ' Tell him,' quoth she, ' my mourning weeds are
        done,
    And I am ready to put armour on.'

K.E. Belike she minds to play the Amazon.
    But what said Warwick to these injuries ?

Post. He, more incens'd against your majesty
    Than all the rest, discharg'd me with these words :
    ' Tell him from me that he hath done me wrong,   110
    And therefore I 'll uncrown him, ere 't be long.'

K.E. Ha ? durst the traitor breathe out so proud words ?

Well, I will arm me, being thus forewarn'd :
They shall have wars, and pay for their presumption.
But say, is Warwick friends with Margaret ?

Post. Ay, gracious sovereign ; they are so link'd in
    friendship,
That young Prince Edward marries Warwick's
    daughter.

Cla. Belike the elder ; Clarence will have the younger.
Now, brother king, farewell, and sit you fast,
For I will hence to Warwick's other daughter ;   120
That, though I want a kingdom, yet in marriage
I may not prove inferior to yourself.
You that love me, and Warwick, follow me.

           Exit Clarence, and Somerset follows

Glo. (*aside*) Not I :   †
My thoughts aim at a further matter ; I
Stay not for the love of Edward, but the crown.

K.E. Clarence and Somerset both gone to Warwick ?
Yet am I arm'd against the worst can happen ;
And haste is needful in this desperate case.
Pembroke and Stafford, you in our behalf   130
Go levy men, and make prepare for war ;
They are already, or quickly will be landed :
Myself in person will straight follow you.

           Exeunt Pembroke and Stafford

But, ere I go, Hastings and Montague,
Resolve my doubt.   You twain, of all the rest,
Are near to Warwick by blood and by alliance :
Tell me if you love Warwick more than me ;
If it be so, then both depart to him ;
I rather wish you foes than hollow friends :
But if you mind to hold your true obedience,   140
Give me assurance with some friendly vow,
That I may never have you in suspect.

Mon. So God help Montague as he proves true !
Has. And Hastings as he favours Edward's cause !
K.E. Now, brother Richard, will you stand by us ?
Glo. Ay, in despite of all that shall withstand you.
K.E. Why, so ! then am I sure of victory.
Now therefore let us hence ; and lose no hour,
Till we meet Warwick, with his foreign power.

Exeunt

SCENE II

A plain in Warwickshire

Enter Warwick and Oxford, with French soldiers

War. Trust me, my lord, all hitherto goes well ;
The common people by numbers swarm to us.

Enter Clarence and Somerset

But see where Somerset and Clarence comes !
Speak suddenly, my lords, are we all friends ?

Cla. Fear not that, my lord.

War. Then, gentle Clarence, welcome unto Warwick ;
And welcome, Somerset : I hold it cowardice
To rest mistrustful where a noble heart
Hath pawn'd an open hand in sign of love ;
Else might I think that Clarence, Edward's brother,   10
Were but a feigned friend to our proceedings :
But welcome, sweet Clarence, my daughter shall be
    thine.
And now what rests but, in night's coverture,
Thy brother being carelessly encamp'd,
His soldiers lurking in the towns about,
And but attended by a simple guard,
We may surprise and take him at our pleasure ?
Our scouts have found the adventure very easy :
That as Ulysses and stout Diomede   †
With sleight and manhood stole to Rhesus' tents,   20
And brought from thence the Thracian fatal steeds,
So we, well cover'd with the night's black mantle,
At unawares may beat down Edward's guard,
And seize himself ; I say not, slaughter him,
For I intend but only to surprise him.

You that will follow me to this attempt,
Applaud the name of Henry with your leader.

They all cry, 'Henry !'

Why, then, let's on our way in silent sort :
For Warwick and his friends, God and Saint George !

Exeunt

SCENE III

Edward's camp, near Warwick

Enter three watchmen, to guard the King's tent

1. *W.*Come on, my masters, each man take his stand :
   The king by this is set him down to sleep.
2. *W.*What, will he not to bed ?
1. *W.*Why, no ; for he hath made a solemn vow
   Never to lie and take his natural rest,
   Till Warwick, or himself, be quite suppress'd.
2. *W.*To-morrow then belike shall be the day,
   If Warwick be so near as men report.
3. *W.*But say, I pray, what nobleman is that,
   That with the king here resteth in his tent ?   10
1. *W.*'Tis the Lord Hastings, the king's chiefest friend.
3. *W.*O, is it so ?   But why commands the king
   That his chief followers lodge in towns about him,

While he himself keeps in the cold field ?

2. *W.*'Tis the more honour, because more dangerous.

3. *W.*Ay, but give me worship, and quietness,
    I like it better than a dangerous honour.
    If Warwick knew in what estate he stands,
    'Tis to be doubted he would waken him.

1. *W.*Unless our halberds did shut up his passage.   20

2. *W.*Ay ; wherefore else guard we his royal tent,
    But to defend his person from night-foes ?

> *Enter Warwick, Clarence, Oxford, Somerset, and*
> *French soldiers, silent all*

*War.*This is his tent, and see where stand his guard.
    Courage, my masters ! honour now or never !
    But follow me, and Edward shall be ours.

1. *W.*Who goes there ?

2. *W.*Stay, or thou diest !

> *Warwick and the rest cry all, 'Warwick ! War-*
> *wick !' and set upon the Guard, who fly,*
> *crying, 'Arm ! arm !' Warwick and the*
> *rest following them*

The drum playing and trumpet sounding, re-enter Warwick,
Somerset, and the rest, bringing the King out in his gown,
sitting in a chair. Richard and Hastings fly over the
stage

Som. What are they that fly there ?

*War.*Richard and Hastings: let them go; here is
The duke.

*K.E.*The duke? Why, Warwick, when we parted,   30
Thou call'dst me king.

War.   Ay, but the case is alter'd:
When you disgrac'd me in my embassade,
Then I degraded you from being king,
And come now to create you Duke of York.
Alas, how should you govern any kingdom,
That know not how to use ambassadors,
Nor how to be contented with one wife,
Nor how to use your brothers brotherly,
Nor how to study for the people's welfare,
Nor how to shroud yourself from enemies?   40

*K.E.*Yea, brother of Clarence, art thou here too?
Nay, then I see that Edward needs must down.
Yet, Warwick, in despite of all mischance,
Of thee thyself and all thy complices,
Edward will always bear himself as king:
Though fortune's malice overthrow my state,
My mind exceeds the compass of her wheel.

*War.*Then, for his mind, be Edward England's king:
                         Takes off his crown
But Henry now shall wear the English crown,
And be true king indeed; thou but the shadow.   50

94

My Lord of Somerset, at my request,
See that forthwith Duke Edward be convey'd
Unto my brother, Archbishop of York.
When I have fought with Pembroke and his fellows,
I'll follow you, and tell what answer
Lewis and the Lady Bona send to him.
Now, for a while farewell, good Duke of York.

They lead him out forcibly

K.E. What fates impose, that men must needs abide;
It boots not to resist both wind and tide.

Exit, guarded

Oxf. What now remains, my lords, for us to do,   60
But march to London with our soldiers?

War. Ay, that's the first thing that we have to do,
To free King Henry from imprisonment,
And see him seated in the regal throne.
[Come, let us haste away, and having pass'd these
      cares,
I'll post to York, and see how Edward fares.]

Exeunt

SCENE IV

London. The palace

Enter Queen Elizabeth and Rivers

Riv. Madam, what makes you in this sudden change ?

Q.E. Why, brother Rivers, are you yet to learn
 What late misfortune is befall'n King Edward ?

Riv. What, loss of some pitch'd battle against Warwick ?

Q.E. No, but the loss of his own royal person.

Riv. Then is my sovereign slain ?

Q.E. Ay, almost slain, for he is taken prisoner,
 Either betray'd by falsehood of his guard,
 Or by his foe surpris'd at unawares :
 And, as I further have to understand,   10
 Is new committed to the Bishop of York,
 Fell Warwick's brother and by that our foe.

Riv. These news I must confess are full of grief,
 Yet, gracious madam, bear it as you may ;
 Warwick may lose, that now hath won the day.

Q.E. Till then fair hope must hinder life's decay.
 And I the rather wean me from despair
 For love of Edward's offspring in my womb :
 This is it that makes me bridle passion,
 And bear with mildness my misfortune's cross ;   20

Ay, ay, for this I draw in many a tear
And stop the rising of blood-sucking sighs,
Lest with my sighs or tears I blast or drown
King Edward's fruit, true heir to the English crown.

Riv. But, madam, where is Warwick then become?

*Q.E.*I am inform'd that he comes towards London,
To set the crown once more on Henry's head:
Guess thou the rest; King Edward's friends must
    down.
But, to prevent the tyrant's violence,—
For trust not him that hath once broken faith,— 30
I'll hence forthwith unto the sanctuary,
To save at least the heir of Edward's right:
There shall I rest secure from force and fraud.
Come, therefore, let us fly, while we may fly:
If Warwick take us, we are sure to die.   *Exeunt*

SCENE V

A park near Middleham Castle in Yorkshire

*Enter Gloucester, Lord Hastings, Sir William Stanley,
and others*

Glo. Now, my Lord Hastings, and Sir William Stanley,
Leave off to wonder why I drew you hither,

Into this chiefest thicket of the park.
Thus stands the case : you know our king, my brother,
Is prisoner to the bishop here, at whose hands
He hath good usage, and great liberty,
And, often but attended with weak guard,
Comes hunting this way to disport himself.
I have advertis'd him by secret means,
That if about this hour he make this way,   10
Under the colour of his usual game,
He shall here find his friends with horse and men
To set him free from his captivity.

    Enter King Edward, and a Huntsman with him

Hun. This way, my lord, for this way lies the game.
K.E. Nay, this way, man, see where the huntsmen stand.
    Now, brother of Gloucester, Lord Hastings, and the
      rest,
    Stand you thus close to steal the bishop's deer ?
Glo. Brother, the time and case requireth haste ;
    Your horse stands ready at the park-corner.
K.E. But whither shall we then ?
Has.   To Lynn, my lord,   20
    And ship 't from thence to Flanders.
Glo. Well guess'd, believe me, for that was my meaning.
K.E. Stanley, I will requite thy forwardness.
Glo. But wherefore stay we ? 'tis no time to talk.

*K.E.*Huntsman, what say'st thou? wilt thou go along?

*Hun.*Better do so than tarry and be hang'd.

Glo. Come then, away, let's ha' no more ado.

*K.E.*Bishop, farewell, shield thee from Warwick's frown;

And pray that I may repossess the crown.   *Exeunt*

SCENE VI

London.   The Tower

Flourish.   Enter King Henry, Clarence, Warwick, Somerset,
young Richmond, Oxford, Montague, and Lieutenant of
the Tower.

*K.H.*Master lieutenant, now that God and friends

Have shaken Edward from the regal seat,

And turn'd my captive state to liberty,

My fear to hope, my sorrows unto joys,

At our enlargement what are thy due fees?

*Lieu.*Subjects may challenge nothing of their sovereigns;

But if an humble prayer may prevail,

I then crave pardon of your majesty.

*K.H.*For what, lieutenant? for well using me?

Nay, be thou sure I'll well requite thy kindness,   10

For that it made my imprisonment a pleasure;

Ay, such a pleasure as incaged birds

³⁹ *h*   99

Conceive, when after many moody thoughts,
At last, by notes of household harmony,
They quite forget their loss of liberty.
But, Warwick, after God, thou set'st me free,
And chiefly therefore I thank God and thee;
He was the author, thou the instrument.
Therefore, that I may conquer fortune's spite
By living low, where fortune cannot hurt me, 20
And that the people of this blessed land
May not be punish'd with my thwarting stars,
Warwick, although my head still wear the crown,
I here resign my government to thee,
For thou art fortunate in all thy deeds.

War. Your grace hath still been fam'd for virtuous,
And now may seem as wise as virtuous,
By spying and avoiding fortune's malice,
For few men rightly temper with the stars:
Yet in this one thing let me blame your grace, 30
For choosing me when Clarence is in place.

Cla. No, Warwick, thou art worthy of the sway,
To whom the heavens in thy nativity
Adjudg'd an olive branch, and laurel crown,
As likely to be blest in peace and war;
And therefore I yield thee my free consent.

War. And I choose Clarence only for protector.

*K.H.*Warwick and Clarence, give me both your hands :
 Now join your hands, and with your hands your
   hearts,
 That no dissension hinder government :   40
 I make you both protectors of this land,
 While I myself will lead a private life,
 And in devotion spend my latter days,
 To sin's rebuke, and my Creator's praise.

*War.*What answers Clarence to his sovereign's will ?

Cla. That he consents, if Warwick yield consent,
 For on thy fortune I repose myself.

*War.*Why, then, though loath, yet must I be content :
 We 'll yoke together, like a double shadow
 To Henry's body, and supply his place ;
 I mean, in bearing weight of government,   50
 While he enjoys the honour, and his ease.
 And, Clarence, now then it is more than needful
 Forthwith that Edward be pronounc'd a traitor,
 And all his lands and goods be confiscate.

Cla. What else ? and that succession be determin'd.

*War.*Ay, therein Clarence shall not want his part.

*K.H.*But, with the first of all your chief affairs,
 Let me entreat, for I command no more,
 That Margaret your queen, and my son Edward, 60
 Be sent for, to return from France with speed ;

For, till I see them here, by doubtful fear
My joy of liberty is half eclips'd.

Cla. It shall be done, my sovereign, with all speed.

K.H. My Lord of Somerset, what youth is that,
Of whom you seem to have so tender care?

Som. My liege, it is young Henry, earl of Richmond.

K.H. Come hither, England's hope. (*Lays his hand on
his head.*)   If secret powers
Suggest but truth to my divining thoughts,
This pretty lad will prove our country's bliss.   70
His looks are full of peaceful majesty,
His head by nature framed to wear a crown,
His hand to wield a sceptre, and himself
Likely in time to bless a regal throne.
Make much of him, my lords, for this is he
Must help you more than you are hurt by me.

Enter a Post

War. What news, my friend?

Post. That Edward is escaped from your brother,
And fled, as he hears since, to Burgundy.

War. Unsavoury news! but how made he escape?   80

Post. He was convey'd by Richard duke of Gloucester,
And the Lord Hastings, who attended him
In secret ambush on the forest side,
And from the bishop's huntsmen rescued him;

      For hunting was his daily exercise.

War. My brother was too careless of his charge.

      But let us hence, my sovereign, to provide

      A salve for any sore that may betide.

             Exeunt all but Somerset, Richmond, and Oxford

Som. My lord, I like not of this flight of Edward's ;

      For doubtless Burgundy will yield him help,   90

      And we shall have more wars before 't be long.

      As Henry's late presaging prophecy

      Did glad my heart, with hope of this young Richmond,

      So doth my heart misgive me, in these conflicts

      What may befall him, to his harm and ours :

      Therefore, Lord Oxford, to prevent the worst,

      Forthwith we 'll send him hence to Brittany,

      Till storms be past of civil enmity.

Oxf. Ay, for if Edward repossess the crown,

      'Tis like that Richmond, with the rest, shall down. 100

Som. It shall be so ; he shall to Brittany.

      Come, therefore, let 's about it speedily.   *Exeunt*

SCENE VII

Before York

*Flourish.   Enter King Edward, Gloucester, Hastings,
and soldiers*

K.E. Now, brother Richard, Lord Hastings, and the rest,
Yet thus far fortune maketh us amends,
And says that once more I shall interchange
My waned state for Henry's regal crown.
Well have we pass'd, and now repass'd, the seas,
And brought desired help from Burgundy :
What then remains, we being thus arriv'd
From Ravenspurgh haven before the gates of York,
But that we enter, as into our dukedom ?

Glo. The gates made fast ?   Brother, I like not this ;   10
For many men that stumble at the threshold
Are well foretold that danger lurks within.

K.E. Tush, man, abodements must not now affright us :
By fair or foul means we must enter in,
For hither will our friends repair to us.

Has. My liege, I'll knock once more to summon them.

*Enter, on the walls, the Mayor of York and his
Brethren*

May. My lords, we were forewarned of your coming,

And shut the gates, for safety of ourselves ;
For now we owe allegiance unto Henry.

K.E. But, master mayor, if Henry be your king,   20
Yet Edward at the least is Duke of York.

May. True, my good lord, I know you for no less.

K.E. Why, and I challenge nothing but my dukedom,
As being well content with that alone.

Glo. (*aside*) But when the fox hath once got in his nose,
He'll soon find means to make the body follow.

Has. Why, master mayor, why stand you in a doubt ?
Open the gates, we are King Henry's friends.

May. Ay, say you so ? the gates shall then be open'd.
They descend

Glo. A wise stout captain, and soon persuaded !   30

Has. The good old man would fain that all were well,
So 'twere not long of him ; but being enter'd,
I doubt not, I, but we shall soon persuade
Both him, and all his brothers, unto reason.

Enter the Mayor and two Aldermen, below

K.E. So, master mayor : these gates must not be shut
But in the night or in the time of war.
What ! fear not, man, but yield me up the keys ;
Takes his keys

For Edward will defend the town and thee,
And all those friends that deign to follow me.

March.   Enter Montgomery, with drum and soldiers

Glo. Brother, this is Sir John Montgomery,   40
    Our trusty friend, unless I be deceiv'd.

K.E. Welcome, Sir John ! But why come you in arms ?

Montgom. To help King Edward in his time of storm,
    As every loyal subject ought to do.

K.E. Thanks, good Montgomery ; but we now forget
    Our title to the crown, and only claim
    Our dukedom, till God please to send the rest.

Montgom. Then fare you well, for I will hence again ;
    I came to serve a king, and not a duke.
    Drummer, strike up, and let us march away.   50

                  The drum begins to march

K.E. Nay, stay, Sir John, a while, and we 'll debate
    By what safe means the crown may be recover'd.

Montgom. What talk you of debating ? in few words,
    If you 'll not here proclaim yourself our king,
    I 'll leave you to your fortune, and be gone,
    To keep them back that come to succour you :
    Why shall we fight, if you pretend no title ?

Glo. Why, brother, wherefore stand you on nice points ?

K.E. When we grow stronger, then we 'll make our claim :
    Till then, 'tis wisdom to conceal our meaning.   60

Has. Away with scrupulous wit, now arms must rule.

Glo. And fearless minds climb soonest unto crowns.

Brother, we will proclaim you out of hand ;
The bruit thereof will bring you many friends.

K.E. Then be it as you will ; for 'tis my right,
And Henry but usurps the diadem.

Montgom. Ay, now my sovereign speaketh like himself,
And now will I be Edward's champion.

Has. Sound trumpet, Edward shall be here proclaim'd :
Come, fellow-soldier, make thou proclamation.   70

Flourish

Sold. Edward the Fourth, by the grace of God, king of
England and France, and lord of Ireland, &c.

Montgom. And whosoe'er gainsays King Edward's right,
By this I challenge him to single fight.

Throws down his gauntlet

All. Long live Edward the Fourth !

K.E. Thanks, brave Montgomery, and thanks unto you
all :
If fortune serve me, I 'll requite this kindness.
Now, for this night, let 's harbour here in York ;
And when the morning sun shall raise his car
Above the border of this horizon,   80
We 'll forward towards Warwick and his mates ;
For well I wot that Henry is no soldier.
Ah, froward Clarence ! how evil it beseems thee,
To flatter Henry, and forsake thy brother !

Yet, as we may, we'll meet both thee and Warwick.
Come on, brave soldiers : doubt not of the day,
And, that once gotten, doubt not of large pay.

Exeunt

SCENE VIII

London.   The palace

*Flourish.   Enter King Henry, Warwick, Montague,
Clarence, Exeter, and Oxford*

*War.*What counsel, lords ?   Edward from Belgia,
With hasty Germans, and blunt Hollanders,
Hath pass'd in safety through the narrow seas,
And with his troops doth march amain to London,
And many giddy people flock to him.

*K.H.*Let's levy men, and beat him back again.

Cla. A little fire is quickly trodden out,
Which, being suffer'd, rivers cannot quench.

*War.*In Warwickshire I have true-hearted friends,
Not mutinous in peace, yet bold in war,   10
Those will I muster up : and thou, son Clarence,
Shalt stir up in Suffolk, Norfolk, and in Kent,
The knights and gentlemen, to come with thee :
Thou, brother Montague, in Buckingham,

Northampton, and in Leicestershire, shalt find
Men well inclin'd to hear what thou command'st:
And thou, brave Oxford, wondrous well belov'd,
In Oxfordshire shalt muster up thy friends.
My sovereign, with the loving citizens,
Like to his island, girt in with the ocean,   20
Or modest Dian, circled with her nymphs,
Shall rest in London, till we come to him.
Fair lords, take leave, and stand not to reply.
Farewell, my sovereign.

K.H. Farewell, my Hector, and my Troy's true hope.

Cla. In sign of truth, I kiss your highness' hand.

K.H. Well-minded Clarence, be thou fortunate!

Mon. Comfort, my lord, and so I take my leave.

Oxf. And thus I seal my truth, and bid adieu.

K.H. Sweet Oxford, and my loving Montague,   30
    And all at once, once more a happy farewell.

War. Farewell, sweet lords, let's meet at Coventry.
                  Exeunt all but King Henry and Exeter

K.H. Here at the palace will I rest a while.
    Cousin of Exeter, what thinks your lordship?
    Methinks the power that Edward hath in field
    Should not be able to encounter mine.

Exe. The doubt is that he will seduce the rest.

K.H. That's not my fear, my meed hath got me fame:

I have not stopp'd mine ears to their demands,
Nor posted off their suits with slow delays;   **40**
My pity hath been balm to heal their wounds,
My mildness hath allay'd their swelling griefs,
My mercy dried their water-flowing tears;
I have not been desirous of their wealth,
Nor much oppress'd them with great subsidies,
Nor forward of revenge, though they much err'd:
Then why should they love Edward more than me?
No, Exeter, these graces challenge grace:
And when the lion fawns upon the lamb,
The lamb will never cease to follow him.   **50**

>   *Shout within, 'A Lancaster! A Lancaster!'*

Exe. Hark, hark, my lord! what shouts are these?

>   *Enter King Edward, Gloucester, and Soldiers*

K.E. Seize on the shame-fac'd Henry, bear him hence;
And once again proclaim us king of England.
You are the fount that makes small brooks to flow;
Now stops thy spring, my sea shall suck them dry,
And swell so much the higher by their ebb.
Hence with him to the Tower, let him not speak.

>   *Exeunt some with King Henry*

And, lords, towards Coventry bend we our course,
Where peremptory Warwick now remains:
The sun shines hot, and if we use delay,   **60**

Cold biting winter mars our hop'd-for hay.
Glo. Away betimes, before his forces join,
And take the great-grown traitor unawares :
Brave warriors, march amain towards Coventry.

Exeunt

Act Fifth

SCENE I

Coventry

Enter Warwick, the Mayor of Coventry, two Messengers,
and others upon the walls

*War.*Where is the post that came from valiant Oxford ?
How far hence is thy lord, mine honest fellow ?
*1.M.*By this at Dunsmore, marching hitherward.
*War.*How far off is our brother Montague ?
Where is the post that came from Montague ?
*2.M.*By this at Daintry, with a puissant troop.

Enter Sir John Somerville

*War.*Say, Somervile, what says my loving son ?
And, by thy guess, how nigh is Clarence now ?
*Som.*At Southam I did leave him with his forces,

And do expect him here some two hours hence.   **10**

Drum heard

*War.*Then Clarence is at hand; I hear his drum.

*Som.*It is not his, my lord, here Southam lies:

The drum your honour hears marcheth from
Warwick.

*War.*Who should that be? belike, unlook'd-for friends.

Som. They are at hand, and you shall quickly know.

*March. Flourish. Enter King Edward, Gloucester,
and Soldiers*

*K.E.*Go, trumpet, to the walls, and sound a parle.

Glo. See how the surly Warwick mans the wall!

*War.*O unbid spite! is sportful Edward come?

Where slept our scouts, or how are they seduc'd,

That we could hear no news of his repair?   **20**

*K.E.*Now, Warwick, wilt thou ope the city gates,

Speak gentle words, and humbly bend thy knee,

Call Edward king, and at his hands beg mercy?

And he shall pardon thee these outrages.

*War.*Nay, rather, wilt thou draw thy forces hence,

Confess who set thee up and pluck'd thee down,

Call Warwick patron, and be penitent?

And thou shalt still remain the Duke of York.

Glo. I thought, at least, he would have said the king;

Or did he make the jest against his will?   **30**

*War.*Is not a dukedom, sir, a goodly gift?

Glo. Ay, by my faith, for a poor earl to give:
    I'll do thee service for so good a gift.

War.'Twas I that gave the kingdom to thy brother.

*K.E.*Why then 'tis mine, if but by Warwick's gift.

*War.*Thou art no Atlas for so great a weight:
    And, weakling, Warwick takes his gift again;
    And Henry is my king, Warwick his subject.

*K.E.*But Warwick's king is Edward's prisoner:
    And, gallant Warwick, do but answer this: 40
    What is the body when the head is off?

Glo. Alas, that Warwick had no more forecast,
    But, whiles he thought to steal the single ten,
    The king was slily finger'd from the deck!
    You left poor Henry at the bishop's palace,
    And, ten to one, you'll meet him in the Tower.

K.E.'Tis even so, yet you are Warwick still.

Glo. Come, Warwick, take the time, kneel down, kneel
      down:
    Nay, when? strike now, or else the iron cools.

*War.*I had rather chop this hand off at a blow,   50
    And with the other fling it at thy face,
    Than bear so low a sail, to strike to thee.

*K.E.*Sail how thou canst, have wind and tide thy friend,
    This hand, fast wound about thy coal-black hair,

Shall, whiles thy head is warm and new cut off,
Write in the dust this sentence with thy blood,
'Wind-changing Warwick now can change no
  more.'

Enter Oxford, with drum and colours

War. O cheerful colours ! see where Oxford comes !
Oxf. Oxford, Oxford, for Lancaster !

He and his forces enter the city

Glo. The gates are open, let us enter too.   60
K.E. So other foes may set upon our backs.
  Stand we in good array ; for they no doubt
  Will issue out again and bid us battle :
  If not, the city being but of small defence,
  We 'll quickly rouse the traitors in the same.
War. O, welcome, Oxford ! for we want thy help.

Enter Montague, with drum and colours

Mon. Montague, Montague, for Lancaster !

He and his forces enter the city

Glo. Thou and thy brother both shall buy this treason
  Even with the dearest blood your bodies bear.
K.E. The harder match'd, the greater victory :   70
  My mind presageth happy gain and conquest.

Enter Somerset, with drum and colours

Som. Somerset, Somerset, for Lancaster !

He and his forces enter the city

Glo. Two of thy name, both Dukes of Somerset,
        Have sold their lives unto the house of York,
        And thou shalt be the third, if this sword hold.

> *Enter Clarence, with drum and colours*

War. And lo, where George of Clarence sweeps along,
        Of force enough to bid his brother battle ;
        With whom an upright zeal to right prevails
        More than the nature of a brother's love !
        Come, Clarence, come ; thou wilt, if Warwick call.   80

Cla. Father of Warwick, know you what this means ?

> *Taking his red rose out of his hat*

        Look here, I throw my infamy at thee :
        I will not ruinate my father's house,
        Who gave his blood to lime the stones together,
        And set up Lancaster.   Why, trow'st thou, Warwick,
        That Clarence is so harsh, so blunt, unnatural,
        To bend the fatal instruments of war
        Against his brother, and his lawful king ?
        Perhaps thou wilt object my holy oath :
        To keep that oath were more impiety   90
        Than Jephthah's, when he sacrificed his daughter.   †
        I am so sorry for my trespass made
        That, to deserve well at my brother's hands,
        I here proclaim myself thy mortal foe,
        With resolution, wheresoe'er I meet thee —

As I will meet thee, if thou stir abroad—
To plague thee, for thy foul misleading me.
And so, proud-hearted Warwick, I defy thee,
And to my brother turn my blushing cheeks.
Pardon me, Edward, I will make amends :   100
And, Richard, do not frown upon my faults,
For I will henceforth be no more unconstant.

K.E. Now welcome more, and ten times more belov'd,
Than if thou never hadst deserv'd our hate.

Glo. Welcome, good Clarence, this is brother-like.

War. O passing traitor, perjur'd and unjust !

K.E. What, Warwick, wilt thou leave the town, and fight ?
Or shall we beat the stones about thine ears ?

War. Alas, I am not coop'd here for defence !
I will away towards Barnet presently,   110
And bid thee battle, Edward, if thou dar'st.

K.E. Yes, Warwick, Edward dares, and leads the way :
Lords, to the field ; Saint George, and victory !

          Exeunt King Edward and his company. March
                  Warwick and his company follow

SCENE II

A field of battle near Barnet

*Alarum and excursions.   Enter King Edward, bringing
forth Warwick wounded*

K.E. So, lie thou there : die thou, and die our fear,
 For Warwick was a bug that fear'd us all.
 Now, Montague, sit fast, I seek for thee,
 That Warwick's bones may keep thine company.

             Exit

War. Ah, who is nigh ? come to me, friend or foe,
 And tell me, who is victor, York or Warwick ?
 Why ask I that ? my mangled body shows,
 My blood, my want of strength, my sick heart shows,
 That I must yield my body to the earth,
 And, by my fall, the conquest to my foe.   10
 Thus yields the cedar to the axe's edge,
 Whose arms gave shelter to the princely eagle,
 Under whose shade the ramping lion slept,
 Whose top-branch overpeer'd Jove's spreading tree,
 And kept low shrubs from winter's powerful wind.
 These eyes, that now are dimm'd with death's black
  veil,
 Have been as piercing as the mid-day sun,

To search the secret treasons of the world :
The wrinkles in my brows, now fill'd with blood,
Were liken'd oft to kingly sepulchres ;   20
For who liv'd king, but I could dig his grave ?
And who durst smile, when Warwick bent his
    brow ?
Lo, now my glory smear'd in dust and blood !
My parks, my walks, my manors that I had,
Even now forsake me ; and of all my lands
Is nothing left me but my body's length.
Why, what is pomp, rule, reign, but earth and dust ?
And, live we how we can, yet die we must.

Enter Oxford and Somerset

Som. Ah, Warwick, Warwick ! wert thou as we are,
We might recover all our loss again :   30
The queen from France hath brought a puissant
    power :
Even now we heard the news : ah, couldst thou fly !
War. Why, then I would not fly.   Ah, Montague,
If thou be there, sweet brother, take my hand,
And with thy lips keep in my soul a while !
Thou lov'st me not ; for, brother, if thou didst,
Thy tears would wash this cold congealed blood,
That glues my lips, and will not let me speak.
Come quickly, Montague, or I am dead.

Som. Ah, Warwick ! Montague hath breathed his last,   40
And to the latest gasp cried out for Warwick,
And said ' Commend me to my valiant brother,'
And more he would have said, and more he spoke,
Which sounded like a clamour in a vault,   †
That mought not be distinguish'd ; but at last
I well might hear, delivered with a groan,
' O, farewell, Warwick ! '

War. Sweet rest his soul !   Fly, lords, and save yourselves,
For Warwick bids you all farewell, to meet in heaven.
                                                      Dies

Oxf. {Away, away, to meet the queen's great power !}   50
[Come, noble Somerset, let's take our horse,
And cause retreat be sounded through the camp,
That all our friends that yet remain alive
May be awarn'd and save themselves by flight :
That done, with them we 'll post unto the queen,
And once more try our fortune in the field.]
                Here they bear away his body.   Exeunt

SCENE III

Another part of the field

*Flourish.   Enter King Edward in triumph ; with
Gloucester, Clarence, and the rest*

K.E. Thus far our fortune keeps an upward course,
And we are grac'd with wreaths of victory.
But, in the midst of this bright-shining day,
I spy a black, suspicious, threatening cloud,
That will encounter with our glorious sun,
Ere he attain his easeful western bed :
I mean, my lords, those powers that the queen
Hath rais'd in Gallia have arriv'd our coast,
And, as we hear, march on to fight with us.

Cla. A little gale will soon disperse that cloud,   10
And blow it to the source from whence it came :
The very beams will dry those vapours up,
For every cloud engenders not a storm.

Glo. The queen is valued thirty thousand strong,
And Somerset, with Oxford, fled to her :
If she have time to breathe, be well assur'd
Her faction will be full as strong as ours.

K.E. We are advertis'd by our loving friends
That they do hold their course toward Tewksbury :

We, having now the best at Barnet field,   20
Will thither straight, for willingness rids way,
{And, as we march, our strength will be augmented
In every county as we go along.
Strike up the drum, cry ' Courage ! ', and away.}
[And in every county as we pass along
Our strengths shall be augmented ; come, let's go,
For if we slack this fair, bright summer's day,
Sharp winter's showers will mar our hope for hay.]

Exeunt

SCENE IV

Plains near Tewksbury

*March.   Enter Queen Margaret, Prince Edward,
Somerset, Oxford, and Soldiers*

Mar. Great lords, wise men ne'er sit and wail their loss,
But cheerly seek how to redress their harms.
What though the mast be now blown overboard,
The cable broke, the holding-anchor lost,
And half our sailors swallow'd in the flood ?
Yet lives our pilot still. Is 't meet that he
Should leave the helm, and like a fearful lad
With tearful eyes add water to the sea,
And give more strength to that which hath too much,

Whiles, in his moan, the ship splits on the rock,　　10
Which industry and courage might have sav'd ?
Ah, what a shame, ah, what a fault were this !
Say Warwick was our anchor ; what of that ?
And Montague our topmast ; what of him ?
Our slaughter'd friends the tackles ; what of these ?
Why, is not Oxford here ? another anchor ?
And Somerset, another goodly mast ?
The friends of France our shrouds and tacklings ?
And, though unskilful, why not Ned and I
For once allow'd the skilful pilot's charge ?　　20
We will not from the helm, to sit and weep,
But keep our course (though the rough wind say no)
From shelves and rocks that threaten us with wreck.
As good to chide the waves as speak them fair.
And what is Edward, but a ruthless sea ?
What Clarence, but a quicksand of deceit ?
And Richard, but a ragged fatal rock ?
All these the enemies to our poor bark.
Say you can swim, alas, 'tis but a while !
Tread on the sand, why, there you quickly sink :　　30
Bestride the rock, the tide will wash you off,
Or else you famish ; that 's a threefold death.
This speak I, lords, to let you understand,
In case some one of you would fly from us,

That there's no hop'd-for mercy with the brothers,
More than with ruthless waves, with sands and rocks.
Why, courage then ! what cannot be avoided
'Twere childish weakness to lament or fear.

Pri. Methinks a woman of this valiant spirit
    Should, if a coward heard her speak these words,   40
    Infuse his breast with magnanimity,
    And make him, naked, foil a man at arms.
    I speak not this as doubting any here ;
    For did I but suspect a fearful man,
    He should have leave to go away betimes,
    Lest in our need he might infect another,
    And make him of like spirit to himself.
    If any such be here—as God forbid !—
    Let him depart before we need his help.

Oxf. Women and children of so high a courage,   50
    And warriors faint, why, 'twere perpetual shame.
    O brave young prince ! thy famous grandfather
    Doth live again in thee : long mayst thou live
    To bear his image, and renew his glories !

Som. And he that will not fight for such a hope,
    Go home to bed, and like the owl by day,
    If he arise, be mock'd and wonder'd at.

Mar. Thanks, gentle Somerset, sweet Oxford, thanks.

Pri. And take his thanks that yet hath nothing else.

Enter a Messenger

Mes. Prepare you, lords, for Edward is at hand,   60
    Ready to fight ; therefore be resolute.

Oxf. I thought no less : it is his policy
    To haste thus fast, to find us unprovided.

Som. But he 's deceiv'd, we are in readiness.

Mar. This cheers my heart, to see your forwardness.

Oxf. Here pitch our battle, hence we will not budge.

*Flourish and March.   Enter King Edward, Gloucester,
Clarence, and Soldiers*

K.E. Brave followers, yonder stands the thorny wood,
    Which, by the heavens' assistance, and your strength,
    Must by the roots be hewn up yet ere night.
    I need not add more fuel to your fire,
    For well I wot ye blaze, to burn them out :   70
    Give signal to the fight, and to it, lords !

Mar. Lords, knights, and gentlemen, what I should say
    My tears gainsay ; for every word I speak,
    Ye see I drink the water of mine eyes.
    Therefore no more but this : Henry, your sovereign
    Is prisoner to the foe, his state usurp'd,
    His realm a slaughter-house, his subjects slain,
    His statutes cancell'd, and his treasure spent ;
    And yonder is the wolf, that makes this spoil.   80

You fight in justice : then, in God's name, lords,
Be valiant, and give signal to the fight.

Alarum : Retreat : Excursions. Exeunt

SCENE V

Another part of the field

{*Flourish. Enter King Edward, Gloucester, Clarence, and
soldiers ; with Queen Margaret, Oxford, and Somerset,
prisoners*}

[*Alarms to the battle, York flies, then the chambers be dis-
charged. Then enter the King, Clarence and Gloucester
and the rest, and make a great shout and cry, ' for York !
for York !', and then the Queen is taken, and the Prince,
and Oxford and Somerset ; and then sound, and enter all
again*]

K.E. Now here a period of tumultuous broils.
  Away with Oxford to Hames Castle straight :
  For Somerset, off with his guilty head.
  Go, bear them hence, I will not hear them speak.
Oxf. For my part, I 'll not trouble thee with words.
Som. Nor I, but stoop with patience to my fortune.

Exeunt Oxford and Somerset, guarded

Mar. So part we sadly in this troublous world,

To meet with joy in sweet Jerusalem.

K.E. Is proclamation made, that who finds Edward
    Shall have a high reward, and he his life ?   10

Glo. It is, and lo, where youthful Edward comes !
        Enter Soldiers, with Prince Edward

K.E. Bring forth the gallant, let us hear him speak.
    What ? can so young a thorn begin to prick ?
    Edward, what satisfaction canst thou make
    For bearing arms, for stirring up my subjects,
    And all the trouble thou hast turn'd me to ?

Pri. Speak like a subject, proud ambitious York !
    Suppose that I am now my father's mouth,
    Resign thy chair, and where I stand, kneel thou,
    Whilst I propose the selfsame words to thee,   20
    Which, traitor, thou wouldst have me answer to.

Mar. Ah, that thy father had been so resolv'd !

Glo. That you might still have worn the petticoat,
    And ne'er have stol'n the breech from Lancaster.

Pri. Let Æsop fable in a winter's night ;
    His currish riddles sorts not with this place.

Glo. By heaven, brat, I'll plague ye for that word.

Mar. Ay, thou wast born to be a plague to men.

Glo. For God's sake, take away this captive scold.

Pri. Nay, take away this scolding crook-back, rather. 30

K.E. Peace, wilful boy, or I will charm your tongue.

Cla. Untutor'd lad, thou art too malapert.

Pri. I know my duty, you are all undutiful :
    Lascivious Edward, and thou perjur'd George,
    And thou mis-shapen Dick, I tell ye all,
    I am your better, traitors as ye are,
    And thou usurp'st my father's right and mine.

K.E. Take that, thou likeness of this railer here.   *Stabs him*

Glo. Sprawl'st thou ? take that, to end thy agony.

                                    Stabs him

Cla. And there's for twitting me with perjury.   *Stabs him*   40

Mar. O, kill me too !

Glo. Marry, and shall.   *Offers to kill her*

K.E. Hold, Richard, hold, for we have done too much.

Glo. Why should she live, to fill the world with words ?

K.E. What ? doth she swoon ? use means for her recovery.

Glo. Clarence, excuse me to the king my brother ;
    I 'll hence to London on a serious matter :
    Ere ye come there, be sure to hear some news.

Cla. What ? what ?

Glo. The Tower, the Tower.   *Exit* †

Mar. O Ned, sweet Ned, speak to thy mother, boy !   51
    Canst thou not speak ?   O traitors, murderers !
    They that stabb'd Cæsar shed no blood at all ;
    Did not offend, nor were not worthy blame,
    If this foul deed were by to equal it :

He was a man; this, in respect, a child,
And men ne'er spend their fury on a child.
What's worse than murderer, that I may name it?
No, no, my heart will burst, an if I speak,
And I will speak, that so my heart may burst.   60
Butchers and villains! bloody cannibals!
How sweet a plant have you untimely cropp'd!
You have no children, butchers! if you had,
The thought of them would have stirr'd up remorse;
But if you ever chance to have a child,
Look in his youth to have him so cut off,
As, deathsmen, you have rid this sweet young prince!

K.E. Away with her, go, bear her hence perforce.

Mar. Nay, never bear me hence, dispatch me here;
Here sheathe thy sword, I'll pardon thee my death: 70
What? wilt thou not? then, Clarence, do it thou.

Cla. By heaven, I will not do thee so much ease.

Mar. Good Clarence, do; sweet Clarence, do thou do it.

Cla. Didst thou not hear me swear I would not do it?

Mar. Ay, but thou usest to forswear thyself:
'Twas sin before, but now 'tis charity.
What, wilt thou not? Where is that devil's butcher,
Hard-favour'd Richard? Richard, where art thou?
Thou art not here: murder is thy alms-deed;
Petitioners for blood thou ne'er put'st back.   80

*K.E.*Away, I say, I charge ye bear her hence.

*Mar.*So come to you, and yours, as to this prince !

Exit, led out forcibly

*K.E.*Where 's Richard gone ?

Cla. To London, all in post, and, as I guess,
To make a bloody supper in the Tower.

*K.E.*He 's sudden, if a thing comes in his head.
Now march we hence, discharge the common sort
With pay and thanks, and let 's away to London,
And see our gentle queen how well she fares ;
By this, I hope, she hath a son for me. *Exeunt* 90

SCENE VI

London.   The Tower

*Enter King Henry and Gloucester, with the Lieutenant,
on the walls*

Glo. Good day, my lord.   What, at your book so hard ?

*K.H.*Ay, my good lord :—my lord, I should say rather ;
'Tis sin to flatter, ' good ' was little better :
' Good Gloucester ' and ' good devil ' were alike,
And both preposterous ; therefore, not ' good lord.'

Glo. Sirrah, leave us to ourselves, we must confer.

Exit Lieutenant

*K.H.*So flies the reckless shepherd from the wolf ;
  So first the harmless sheep doth yield his fleece,
  And next his throat, unto the butcher's knife.
  What scene of death hath Roscius now to act ?   **10**

Glo. Suspicion always haunts the guilty mind ;
  The thief doth fear each bush an officer.

*K.H.*The bird that hath been limed in a bush,
  With trembling wings misdoubteth every bush ;
  And I, the hapless male to one sweet bird,
  Have now the fatal object in my eye,
  Where my poor young was lim'd, was caught, and
    kill'd.

Glo. Why, what a peevish fool was that of Crete,
  That taught his son the office of a fowl !
  And yet, for all his wings, the fool was drown'd.   **20**

*K.H.*I Dædalus, my poor boy Icarus,   †
  Thy father Minos, that denied our course,
  The sun that sear'd the wings of my sweet boy
  Thy brother Edward, and thyself the sea
  Whose envious gulf did swallow up his life.
  Ah, kill me with thy weapon, not with words !
  My breast can better brook thy dagger's point,
  Than can my ears that tragic history.
  But wherefore dost thou come ? is 't for my life ?

Glo. Think'st thou I am an executioner ?   **30**

K.H. A persecutor, I am sure, thou art,
   If murdering innocents be executing,
   Why, then thou art an executioner.

Glo. Thy son I kill'd for his presumption.

K.H. Hadst thou been kill'd when first thou didst presume,
   Thou hadst not liv'd to kill a son of mine.
   And thus I prophesy, that many a thousand,
   Which now mistrust no parcel of my fear,
   And many an old man's sigh, and many a widow's,
   And many an orphan's water-standing eye,   40
   Men for their sons, wives for their husbands,
   And orphans for their parents' timeless death,
   Shall rue the hour that ever thou wast born.
   The owl shriek'd at thy birth, an evil sign,
   The night-crow cried, aboding luckless time,
   Dogs howl'd, and hideous tempest shook down
     trees ;
   The raven rook'd her on the chimney top,
   And chattering pies in dismal discords sung ;
   Thy mother felt more than a mother's pain,
   And yet brought forth less than a mother's hope, 50
   To wit, an indigested and deformed lump,
   Not like the fruit of such a goodly tree.
   Teeth hadst thou in thy head when thou wast born,
   To signify thou cam'st to bite the world :

And, if the rest be true, which I have heard,
Thou cam'st—.

Glo. I 'll hear no more : die, prophet, in thy speech :

Stabs him

For this, amongst the rest, was I ordain'd.

K.H. Ay, and for much more slaughter after this :
O, God forgive my sins, and pardon thee !   *Dies* 60

Glo. What ? will the aspiring blood of Lancaster
Sink in the ground ? I thought it would have
    mounted.
See how my sword weeps for the poor king's death.
O, may such purple tears be alway shed
From those that wish the downfall of our house !
If any spark of life be yet remaining,
Down, down to hell, and say I sent thee thither :

Stabs him again

I, that have neither pity, love, nor fear,
Indeed, 'tis true that Henry told me of ;
For I have often heard my mother say   70
I came into the world with my legs forward :
Had I not reason, think ye, to make haste,
And seek their ruin that usurp'd our right ?
The midwife wonder'd, and the women cried
' O, Jesus bless us, he is born with teeth ! '
And so I was ; which plainly signified

That I should snarl, and bite, and play the dog.
Then, since the heavens have shap'd my body so,
Let hell make crook'd my mind to answer it.
[I had no father, I am like no father,]
I have no brother, I am like no brother;   80
And this word 'love,' which greybeards call divine,
Be resident in men like one another,
And not in me: I am myself alone.
Clarence, beware, thou keep'st me from the light,
But I will sort a pitchy day for thee;
For I will buz abroad such prophecies
That Edward shall be fearful of his life,
And then, to purge his fear, I'll be thy death.
King Henry, and the prince his son, are gone;
Clarence, thy turn is next, and then the rest,   90
Counting myself but bad till I be best.
I'll throw thy body in another room,
And triumph, Henry, in thy day of doom.

                                    Exit, with the body

SCENE VII

London.   The palace

Flourish.   Enter King Edward, Queen Elizabeth, Clarence,
Gloucester, Hastings, a Nurse wth the young Prince,
and Attendants.

K.E. Once more we sit in England's royal throne,
Re-purchas'd with the blood of enemies.
What valiant foemen, like to autumn's corn,
Have we mow'd down in tops of all their pride !
Three Dukes of Somerset, threefold renown'd,
For hardy and undoubted champions ;
Two Cliffords, as the father and the son,
And two Northumberlands ; two braver men
Ne'er spurr'd their coursers at the trumpet's sound :
With them, the two brave bears, Warwick and
　　　Montague,　　　　　　　　　　　　　　　　　10
That in their chains fetter'd the kingly lion,
And made the forest tremble when they roar'd.
Thus have we swept suspicion from our seat,
And made our footstool of security.
Come hither, Bess, and let me kiss my boy.
Young Ned, for thee, thine uncles and myself
Have in our armours watch'd the winter's night,

Went all afoot in summer's scalding heat,
That thou mightst repossess the crown in peace :
And of our labours thou shalt reap the gain.   20

Glo. (*aside*) I'll blast his harvest, if your head were laid,
For yet I am not look'd on in the world.
This shoulder was ordain'd so thick, to heave,
And heave it shall some weight, or break my back :
Work thou the way,—and thou shalt execute.

K.E. Clarence and Gloucester, love my lovely queen,
And kiss your princely nephew, brothers both.

Cla. The duty that I owe unto your majesty
I seal upon the lips of this sweet babe.

Q.E. Thanks, noble Clarence, worthy brother, thanks.   30

Glo. And, that I love the tree from whence thou sprang'st,
Witness the loving kiss I give the fruit.
(*aside*) To say the truth, so Judas kiss'd his master,
And cried, ' all hail ! ', when as he meant all harm.

K.E. Now am I seated as my soul delights,
Having my country's peace and brothers' loves.

Cla. What will your grace have done with Margaret ?
Reignier, her father, to the King of France
Hath pawn'd the Sicils and Jerusalem,
And hither have they sent it for her ransom.   40

K.E. Away with her, and waft her hence to France.
And now what rests, but that we spend the time

With stately triumphs, mirthful comic shows,
Such as befits the pleasure of the court ?
Sound drums and trumpets ! farewell sour annoy !
For here, I hope, begins our lasting joy.

Exeunt

Notes

I. i. 78. *as the earldom was*; so F.   Q reads *as the kingdom is*.

I. i. 186. *unmanly*; so F.   Q reads *unkingly*.

I. ii. 6. *slight*; so F.   Q reads *sweet*.

I. iii. 33. *alive*; so F.   Q reads *on earth*, perhaps with a better contrast to *in hell*.

I. iii. 52. *Congeal'd with this*; so F.   Q reads *Congeal'd with his*.

I. iv. 33. *Phaëthon*, the son of the sun-god tried to drive the chariot of the sun, but could not control the horses, came too near the earth, which was scorched, and was himself hurled from the chariot.

I. iv. 95 (S.D.). The justification for this stage-direction (which is in neither text) is Halle's chronicle (as also *Richard III*, I. iii. 175).

I. iv. 137. *O tiger's heart . . .*; this is the line adapted by Greene, in his famous attack in the 'Groatsworth of Wit,' as *Tiger's hart wrapt in a Player's hyde*.

I. iv. 148. *for his death*; so F.   Q reads *as it falls*.

I. iv. 155. *Hyrcania*; so F.   Q reads, most inappositely, *Arcadia*, presumably an actor's, rather than an auditory, error.

II. i. 24. (S.D.). It is clear from the chronicles that this was supposed to be a real appearance and not an illusion, so that the Q stage-direction may be admitted.

II. i. 51, 53. *the hope of Troy* was Hector. There is a Latin proverb, *Ne Hercules quidem contra duos*.

II. i. 127. *captives*; so F.   Q reads *captains*, and though that would be an easy enough actor's error there is a good deal to be said for it.

II. i. 131. *an idle*; so Q, which has here to be invoked to correct the repetition of F, *a lazy*.

II. ii. 25. *unloving*; so F.   Q reads, more pointedly, *unnatural*.

II. ii. 133 (speech-heading) *Rich.*; so Q.   F gives *War.*, which is proved wrong by the Queen's retort.

II. ii. 143. *To let . . . heart*; so F.   But the straightforward contrast of Q seems preferable, *To parley thus with England's lawful heirs.*

II. iv.   This short scene is interesting from the textual point of view, and it is perhaps worth giving the whole of it as it appears in Q.   It will be seen that it starts with a speech of Richard's that reads like a parody, that Clifford's speech is almost identical, and that Richard's final two lines disappear altogether.

> Alarms, and then enter Richard at one door and Clifford at the other.
>
> Rich. *A Clifford, a Clifford.*
> Cli.   *A Richard, a Richard.*
> Rich. *Now Clifford, for York and young Rutland's death*
>   *This thirsty sword that longs to drink thy blood*
>   *Shall lop thy limbs, and slice thy cursed heart,*
>   *For to revenge the murders thou hast made.*
> Cli.   *Now Richard, I am with thee here alone;*
>   *This is the hand that stabb'd thy father York,*
>   *And this the hand that slew thy brother Rutland,*
>   *And here's the heart that triumphs in their deaths,*
>   *And cheers these hands that slew thy sire and brother,*
>   *To execute the like upon thyself;*
>   *And so have at thee!*
> Alarms.   They fight, and then enters Warwick and rescues Richard, and then exeunt omnes.

II. vi. 6. *thy tough commixture*; so F.   Q reads *that tough commixture*.

II. vi. 8, 17. The usual editorial practice has been to give both lines. The mere repetition is not any strong argument against it, since it could be paralleled, but I do not see that the conflation is justified; and it is worth noticing that *York* ends the preceding line in both places.

II. vi. 82. *This hand* . . .; so F, unmetrically. Q reads simply *I'ld cut it off, and with the issuing blood.* F gives the more vivid picture. Perhaps we should omit *issuing* from F's reading.

III. i. (S.D.). As in the similar passage in the Second part (IV. iii.) Q gives us just the characters, two keepers. F however gives us Sinklo and Humfrey, presumably the two actors, John Sincler and Humphrey Jeffes (though why one of them goes under his surname and the other under his Christian name suggests interesting conjectures).

III. i. 24. *thee, sour adversity*; the accepted emendation for F's *the sour adversaries.* The emendation is not particularly easy, but F appears to make no sense.

III. ii. 156. *wither'd shrub*; so F. Q reads, somewhat surprisingly, *wither'd shrimpe*, and Q 3 does not appear to have felt any difficulty about that reading, which one must do the justice of comparing with the *writhled shrimpe* of Part 1, II. iii. 23. I should suspect *shrub*, which when one comes to think it out is not particularly apposite, of being a sophisticating correction of F, if it were not for *Richard III*, III. iv. 12, where Richard speaks of his arm as a *blasted sapling*.

III. ii. 188, 190. *Nestor* was reputed the wisest of the Greeks before Troy, and an eloquent (if long-winded) orator; *Sinon* persuaded the Trojans to take the wooden horse into the city.

III. ii. 192, 193. *Proteus* could change himself into any shape at will; *Machiavelli*, author of *The Prince*, seems to have been to the

Elizabethans a type of one who advocated murder as a method of cold-blooded policy.

III. iii. 127. *Exempt from envy, but not from disdain*; this has caused much trouble. The second half of the line seems clear enough. His love can be blighted by disdain, if the Lady Bona disdains it. But why it should (or not) be exempt from envy (which commonly means simply hatred or ill-will in Shakespeare) I do not know.

IV. i. 124-49. Here again it is interesting to notice the different version of Q, with the omission of Richard's aside, but the addition of three characteristic sardonic lines, and the preparation for Edward in his tent in the next two scenes.

> *Exit Clarence and Somerset*

Edw.*Clarence and Somerset fled to Warwick.*
　　What say you brother Richard, will you stand to us?

Rich.*Ay, my lord, in despite of all that shall withstand you.*
　　For why hath Nature made me halt downright
　　But that I should be valiant and stand to it?
　　For if I would I cannot run away.

Edw.*Pembroke, go raise an army presently;*
　　Pitch up my tent, for in the field this night
　　I mean to rest, and on the morrow morn
　　I'll march to meet proud Warwick ere he land
　　Those straggling troops that he hath got in France.
　　But ere I go, Montague and Hastings,
　　You of all the rest are nearest allied
　　In blood to Warwick; tell me therefore if
　　You favour him more than me or not;
　　Speak truly, for I had rather have you open
　　Enemies than hollow friends.

Mon.*So God help Montague as he proves true.*
Has. *And Hastings as he favours Edward's cause.*
Edw.*It shall suffice; come then let 's march away.*

Exeunt omnes

IV. ii. 19. *Ulysses and stout Diomede*; see *Iliad* x. Rhesus, prince of Thrace, came to aid Troy. The oracle declared that if his horses were watered at the river Xanthus and grazed on the Trojan pastures, Troy would not fall. Ulysses and Diomed penetrated Rhesus' camp on the night of his arrival, killed him, and carried off the horses.

V. ii. 44. *clamour in a vault*; so Q, usually adopted instead of F's *canon in a vault*. Hart protests against the change, but the point is surely the confusion of articulate sound by the echoes of the vault, not merely the reverberations of a shot, which is inarticulate anyway.

V. v. 50. *The Tower, the Tower*; so F. Q makes the meaning perhaps needlessly explicit by reading *The Tower, man, the Tower; I'll root them out.*

V. vi. 21-5. Dædalus designed the labyrinth for Minos, king of Crete. Being kept captive by him he made wings of wax and feathers for himself and his son Icarus, and escaped. Icarus flew too near the sun, the wax melted, and he fell into the sea.

V. i. 91. *Jephthah;* Judges xi. 30–40.

141

Glossary

MANY words and phrases in Shakespeare require glossing, not because they are in themselves unfamiliar, but for the opposite reason, that Shakespeare uses in their Elizabethan and unfamiliar sense a large number of words which seem so familiar that there is no incentive to look for them in the glossary. It is hoped that a glossary arranged as below will make it easy to see at a glance what words and phrases in any particular scene require elucidation. A number of phrases are glossed by what seems to be, in their context, the modern equivalent rather than by lexicographical glosses on the words which compose them.

Act First

SCENE I

line
12 BEAVER, helmet
15 BATTLES, lines of battle
25 FEARFUL, frightened
46 HOLDS UP, upholds
47 BELLS, *i.e.* of the hawk
110 SITH, since
126 DESCENT, descended

line
186 BANDS, bonds
211 BEWRAY, betray
243 WHICH, who
 SILLY, simple
245 GRANTED, assented
268 EMPTY, hungry
269 TIRE, raven

SCENE II

43 WITTY, knowledgeable
48 POST, haste

74 WHENAS, when

SCENE III

48 DI FACIANT LAUDIS SUMMA SIT
 ISTA TUÆ, May the gods
 grant that that be the height
 of your praise

SCENE IV

line
12 FALCHION, sword
19 BODG'D, gave way
29 BUTT, target
34 PRICK, mark on the dial
50 BUCKLE, interchange
60 IMPEACH, slur
61 GIN, trap
62 CONY, rabbit
68 RAUGHT, reached
73 MESS, table of four (*partie carré*)

line
74 LUSTY, lustful
103 PALE, ring
110 ORISONS, prayers
114 TRULL, harlot
121 TYPE, title
122 SICILS, Sicilies (*i.e. Naples and Sicily*)
125 BOOTS, profits
136 SEPTENTRION, north
146 ALLAYS, moderates

Act Second

SCENE I

10 BECOME, ' got to '
14 NEAT, cattle
25 DAZZLE, *intrans.*
27 RACKING CLOUDS, ' cloud-rack '
36 MEEDS, merits
40 TARGET, shield
46 WHENAS, when
71 FOR, on account of
90 CHAIR, ducal throne
106 SITH, since

109 POSTS, messengers
118 DASH, quash
124 HEATED SPLEEN, ardent courage
147 NEEDFUL, wanting support
150 HIS SCANDAL OF RETIRE, scandal of his retiring
169 NAUGHT, haughty
170 MOE, more (*Eliz. plur.*)
193 DEGREE, step
209 SORTS, suits

SCENE II

19 LEVEL, aim
38 FONDLY, foolishly
44 INFERRING, advancing
46 EVER, always
64 APPARENT, heir
66 TOWARD, promising

72 DARRAIGN, array
85 MINIONS, favourites
110-111 REFRAIN THE EXECUTION, restrain the outburst in action
124 RESOLV'D, sure

Act II   Sc. ii—*continued*

line	line
136 STIGMATIC, branded deformity	145 CALLET, wanton
142 SHAM'ST, *intrans.*	152 MATCH'D, mated
EXTRAUGHT, descended	162 SLIPP'D, deferred
143 DETECT, *trans.*	

SCENE III

38 STANDS, suits	56 FORSLOW, delay

SCENE V

3 BLOWING OF HIS NAILS, *i.e.* to keep *his fingers warm*	64 PRESS'D, *i.e.* by pressgang
24 QUAINTLY, skilfully	104 TAKE ON WITH ME, 'go for me'
36 EAN, bear	108 MISTHINK, think amiss of
43 SILLY, simple	118 OBSEQUIOUS, engaged in mourning
50 SECURE, free of care	
53 CURIOUS, elaborate	123 OVERGONE, overwhelmed

SCENE VI

7 MISPROUD, wrongly proud	35 FRETTING, driving
14 SWAY'D, ruled	36 ARGOSY, merchant ship (*orig. of Ragusa*)
24 HOLD, endure	
28 EFFUSE, effusion	42 HER, its (*in O.E. soul is fem.*)

Act Third

SCENE I

1 BRAKE, thicket	13 OF, because of
2 LAUND, plain	71 APPREHEND, arrest

SCENE II

14 KEEP THE WIND, keep to windward (hence driving game into trap)	77 SADNESS, seriousness
	85 WIT, good sense
	107 GHOSTLY, spiritual

Act III Sc. ii—*continued*

line
107 SHRIFT, absolution
108 FOR SHIFT, as a device (*with pun on sense of female garment*)
122 APPREHENSION, arrest
139 LADE, bale
150 WITCH, charm

line
171 IMPALED, circled
187 BASILISK, serpent reputed to kill with glance of eye
192 FOR ADVANTAGES, as it serves my turn

SCENE III

25 OF A KING, from a king
78 INJURIOUS, insulting
99 BUCKLER, shield
128 QUIT HIS PAIN, requite his trouble
136 JOINTURE, marriage settlement
160 CONVEYANCE, trick
162 POST, messenger
189 IMPALE, circle

210 MATCHING, mating
222 IN POST, in haste
226 FEAR, frighten
228 WILLOW GARLAND, traditional mourning wear
235 BID, offer
254 I LONG, I am not content
260 STALE, decoy

Act Fourth

SCENE I

13 ABUSE, trick

107 INJURIES, insults

SCENE II

21 FATAL, involved in decrees of fates

27 APPLAUD, cry out

SCENE IV

1 MAKES YOU IN THIS SUDDEN CHANGE, causes you suddenly to change thus

25 BECOME, 'got to'

SCENE VII

SCENE VIII

Act Fifth

SCENE I

SCENE II

SCENE III

SCENE V

SCENE VI